From Duck Lake
to Dawson City

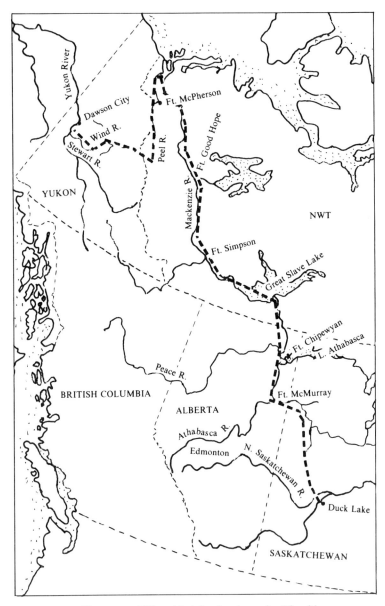

The route of Eben McAdam's trip to the Klondike

From Duck Lake to Dawson City

The Diary of Eben McAdam's
Journey to the Klondike
1898-1899

Edited by R. G. Moyles

Western Producer Prairie Books
Saskatoon, Saskatchewan

Copyright © 1977 R. G. Moyles
Western Producer Prairie Books
Saskatoon, Saskatchewan

Illustration on page 115 from *A Dictionary of Canadianisms*. Reprinted by permission of Gage Educational Publishing Ltd. Care has been taken to credit all copyright material. The publisher will rectify any omissions in future editions.

Cover designed by Dianne Bersea

Printed in Canada by
MODERN PRESS
1
Saskatoon, Saskatchewan

Canadian Cataloguing in Publication Data

McAdam, Ebenezer, 1859-1927.
  From Duck Lake to Dawson City

  Includes index. ✓
  ISBN 0-919306-88-8 ✓

  1. McAdam, Ebenezer, 1859-1927. 2. Yukon
Territory - Description and travel - To 1900.*
3. Klondike gold fields. I. Moyles, Robert
G., 1939- II. Title.
FC4017.1.M23 971.9'1'020924 C77-002207-3
F1091

Preface

Ebenezer McAdam's diary, though not unique, is one of a small number of such diaries; most of the men who went to the Klondike in search of gold were too intent on getting there to take time to record the effort. Many were either too uneducated or too insensitive to realize the historical significance of the occasion. McAdam certainly was not. Though his object was to find gold and, perhaps, even to make a fortune, he was not unaware that both the moment and the method were important enough to leave on record. That record, his personal diary, like all diaries, is an account of personal achievement, but it also contains enough universal human elements — hardship, companionship and conflict — and reveals so much of the historical drama of the Klondike that its publication is warranted.

To enhance it as a readable document I have taken every opportunity afforded by McAdam's comments to amplify, explain and enliven aspects of the journey and of the Klondike goldrush. For example, travelling the same route as McAdam was a former mayor of Hamilton, A. D. Stewart, who also kept a diary up to the week of his death (Stewart died of scurvy at Wind City.) The memoirs of yet another fellow-traveller, George Mitchell, were written up by Angus Graham in a book entitled *The Golden Grindstone.* Excerpts from these and other sources provide excellent additional background material to McAdam's diary. And the whole is further vivified by maps which chart the party's progress and by numerous photographs from McAdam's own collection and from other sources.

Of the diarist himself, Ebenezer McAdam, we know only very little. What we do know is that he was born in Montreal on January 2, 1859, and, in 1885, was married to Ednah Brainard of Boston who bore him two daughters. Very shortly after the birth of her second daughter, Ednah Brainard McAdam died and it was not long after this event that Eben, after sending his two young children to live with his parents-in-law, made his trip to the Klondike. McAdam's eldest daughter, Linda, who donated her father's diary and photo collection to the University of Alberta, states that he had a great love of reading, "an interest in science . . . and a great skill in handiwork." McAdam's diary substantiates that statement; to alleviate the monotony of the long winter nights on the Wind River he gave lectures on the heavenly bodies and carved inscriptions and designs on the rifles of his companions. His diary also gives us some insight into his personality and, quite obviously, lets us know that he did indeed reach Dawson City. What we know of his career after he reached the goldfields will be outlined in a brief epilogue after the last entry in the diary. What little we know about his companions will also be included in that epilogue.

The "McAdam Collection" housed in the special collections unit at the University of Alberta includes three handwritten diaries of his trip to the Klondike, a typed diary of a trip from Fairbanks, Alaska to Dawson City in 1906-07, some gold nuggets, medals, coins, the leg bone of a mammoth found near the mouth of the Peace River in 1898, an Indian basket and hunting knife, and approximately 250 photographs; a few of the photographs are of his trip but most depict life in the Yukon during and after the goldrush. It is an extremely interesting collection, of which the diaries and photographs are the chief items of public interest, and the University of Alberta must be thanked for allowing me to make them public. My sincere thanks, therefore, to Bruce Peel, the University Librarian, and to John Charles, Head of Special Collections, for their interest and cooperation. My thanks also to Maureen Bradbury and Carolyn Poon of Special Collections for their graciousness and to Wanda Chawrun who typed the manuscript. Any errors in either the transcription or the annotations are entirely my own and I welcome further information about any of the people, events and places mentioned.

Introduction

In the winter of 1897 five Montrealers — Andrew Smith, Henry Chomiere, Charles Maltby, Plenderleath McGinnis and Ebenezer McAdam — all became infected by "Klondicitus" or, as the condition was more familiarly known, "the Klondike fever." The symptoms of that "fever" (a lust for gold, an accompanying thirst for adventure, dreams of instant wealth, visions of El Dorado) were nothing new, of course; they had plagued and motivated men without number from time immemorial, men such as Jason, Cortez, Raleigh and Columbus. The Klondike variety was simply a special strain, brought on by the mind-boggling dimensions of the gold strikes being reported from Canada's Yukon Territory since the middle of 1897. After the news of George Carmack's jackpot discovery on Bonanza Creek, tens of thousands (reportedly as many as 100,000) men and women, from all over the world, became infected by that fever; like them, the five Montrealers pooled their resources, outfitted themselves for Arctic survival and, in the spring of 1898, left the relative comfort of the old city to seek their fortunes in the already famous and somewhat fabulous Klondike goldfields.

The rapidity with which the Klondike's fame and fables spread, in that pre-television era, is truly staggering; in a matter of weeks news of the strikes was flashing around the world and stories of lucky prospectors — many of the stories grossly exaggerated — created a Klondike mythology which found instant acceptance in the popular literature of the time.[1] ("The streets of Dawson City," stated the Montreal *Star*, "are literally

1. For a more detailed and colorful account of the manner in which the "fever" spread see Pierre Berton, *Klondike* (Toronto, 1958).

1

paved with gold.") It was, in fact, virtually impossible for any but the most dedicated recluse to have escaped hearing or reading about the Klondike and thus from becoming, to some degree at least, infected by the fever.[2] Canadian and world newspapers, in almost every issue for nigh on two years, fed that fever with incessant Klondike news and editorials.

Take the Montreal newspapers, for example, which Eben McAdam and his partners certainly would have read. The *Star*, the most aggressive of the lot, provided what amounted to a play-by-play account of activities in the Yukon and of the controversies which the goldrush generated in the Canadian Parliament. On February 9, 1898, in a typical issue, the paper carried a four-column report on the parliamentary debate over the proposed Mann-Mackenzie railroad to the headwaters of the Yukon River (the *Star*, being Conservative, was of course opposed to the scheme), described the Chatfield party which was passing through Montreal on its way to the Klondike, showed Mrs. Alice Rollins Crane in Klondike garb, reported that even the Rothschilds had bought a claim, discussed various routes and carried ads for the "Yukonite" (a boat that would take people there), and for various kinds of Klondike outfits.[3] A few days later, on February 12, a special "Klondike Number" contained a lengthy history of the Yukon, magnified its gold resources, provided "do's and don'ts" for the would-be prospector, offered maps and minutely-detailed descriptions of the routes, and concluded with this fence-straddling bit of advice: "The *Star* would not encourage anyone to leave a comfortable home upon the mere chance of making a fortune, nor would it discourage hardy, adventurous spirits from trying the quick road to wealth."

The Montreal *Gazette* and the *Family Herald*, though not quite so vociferous as the *Star*, were not far behind their counterpart in promoting the Klondike myths. Like newspapers throughout the world, they had embellished the already-sensational stories concerning the fabulous fortunes being made — the tales of those first "lucky strikes" and of the wheelbarrows full of gold being unloaded in the port of Seattle.[4] At the time

2. "It was found," stated one Klondiker, "that the symptoms appeared in their most acute form between the hours of six and seven in the evening, when the toils of the day were over and the infected subject had really nothing on his mind, even the problem of what to have for dinner being still comfortably remote." (Angus Graham, *The Golden Grindstone: The Adventures of George M. Mitchell* [London, 1936], p. 3).

3. This railroad remained nothing more than a dream — surveys were made, twelve miles were built, tickets were sold, but it all fell through.

4. See Pierre Berton, *Klondike*, chapter three.

Eben McAdam was preparing to leave for the Klondike, they were carrying such headlines as these: "Reports are decidedly rosy. $9 per pan on Rosebud Creek"; "Rush to the Klondike: CPR train with 3,000 gold seekers on it passed through Toronto"; "Sound Advice from Skagway. How to make a Fortune." These were the stories, then, in addition to the oral tales, which spread the Klondike fever so that men like McAdam, Chomiere, McGinnis, Maltby and Smith — men from all walks of life — left their families and jobs, and set off, with no real knowledge of the road ahead, to seek their "pot of gold" in the Yukon.

Before leaving, however, in their lucid moments, Klondikers such as McAdam were forced to consider some important practical questions, one of the chief being which route to take. The most popular route was the one which, from looking at a map, also seemed easiest to travel: up the British Columbia coast to Skagway, inland via the White or Chilcoot Passes and down a series of lakes and rivers to Dawson City. But, as many men found out, maps can be very deceptive: thousands of dead packhorses and many more thousands of discouraged miners testified to the awful toll which those steep, narrow mountain inclines exacted from those impatient men. "The inhumanity which this trail has been witness to," wrote Major Walsh of the Northwest Mounted Police, "the heartbreak and suffering which so many have undergone, cannot be imagined. They certainly cannot be described."[5] Less impatient men were content with the less arduous all-water route from Vancouver (or perhaps Seattle), 2,700 miles to St. Michael in Alaska and from there 1,700 miles up the Yukon River by steamer. More than ninety percent of all the fevered men and women who swept into the Klondike at the peak of the famous goldrush chose to travel by one of those two routes.

But there were a few — almost 2,000 others — who decided to try one of the "all-Canadian" routes: (1) the overland route northwest from Edmonton, through the Peace River District from where one could fork into a number of alternate river routes to the Yukon; (2) the water route which followed the well-worn Hudson Bay Company route from Athabasca Landing, where steamboats made regular trips downstream to Fort MacMurray, on to Fort Chipewyan, to Great Slave Lake, down the Mackenzie River to Fort McPherson from where several river systems could be ascended to bridge the mountains into the

---

5. Quoted in Berton, *Klondike*, page 155. Chapters four and seven of Berton's book offer vivid pictures of the conditions on those trails.

heart of the Klondike.⁶ It was the second of these, with a slight diversion, that the five Montrealers took and, again, it is not farfetched to suggest that newspaper reports strongly influenced that decision.

Many Eastern-Canadian newspapers, in fact, had come out wholly in support of the "all-Canadian" routes. The Hamilton *Spectator,* for example, not only advocated the Edmonton-Mackenzie water route, but declared that Alderman J. M. Findley and eight other Hamiltonians were leaving for Edmonton to try the route themselves. The Montreal *Star,* in February of 1898, reported that the noted M. P. Frank Oliver and the mayor of Winnipeg, A. J. Jackson, were both in town promoting Edmonton and the Edmonton routes; it also noted that the Montreal Board of Trade (certainly an influential body) had unequivocally endorsed those routes. "It would seem," the *Star* commented, "that a very considerable proportion of the miners going into the Yukon and Northwest Territory are going by way of Edmonton."

That was hardly true, of course, for most were still going in via the Pacific routes and not all those who chose the "all-Canadian" routes were using Edmonton as their terminus: there were a few — a mere handful — who considered it more practical to enter the "wilds" from the vicinity of Prince Albert, Saskatchewan. For after all, as the Prince Albert *Times* made clear (and the Montreal *Star* affirmed), "from Winnipeg to Edmonton by way of Calgary is 1,030 miles, while to Prince Albert is only 603 miles." And when it was further pointed out that from Green Lake, just 150 miles from Prince Albert, "the route is entirely by water with the exception of a few short portages," it must have seemed most attractive. At least we can assume that it did seem so to Eben McAdam and his partners, for that is the route they chose, using Duck Lake, Saskatchewan instead of Edmonton as their point of departure.

Thus the route was chosen. The fact that no one knew anything about the country they would travel through — that without the knowledgeable assistance of Indians and Hudson's Bay factors they would probably never reach the Klondike — was of no concern at the moment. The hardships and realities of the trek itself were some months in the future. Before leaving, another equally important matter had to be attended to: that of provisions — how did one survive in a land devoid of all

---

6. J. G. MacGregor's admirable book, *The Klondike Rush Through Edmonton* (Toronto, 1970), tells the stories of many who travelled those routes.

civilized amenities? what did one take along? how much was enough for a year's travel?

William Ogilvie, official land surveyor and explorer for the Department of the Interior, publisher of *The Klondike Official Guide* (January, 1898), had travelled through most of the Canadian Northwest. Here is his advice regarding supplies:

> For the information of those who have never been in that country I give some notes on the amount of provisions required, first stating that you will require at least 50 per cent more in that region than you would in a more southern latitude. The cold suffered (often intense) for at least seven months in the year conduces to a vigorous appetite. This is a provision of nature, for in order to keep warm the human system has to pile on fuel just as much as any other apparatus where heat is required. . . . The articles that should be taken are:
>
> Of flour we require at least 450 pounds for a year's consumption. This should be of fairly good grade. It need not necessarily be fine flour, but should be good medium. Oatmeal or rolled oats, 50 pounds; cornmeal, 25 pounds. This latter I do not consider so necessary as oatmeal, as oatmeal is a warming food. Bacon (good fat), 250 pounds; hams, 50 pounds; evaporated dried apples, 25 pounds; dried peaches, 25 pounds and if you have a fancy for any other kind of dried fruits you can take them along, or substitute them for one or other of the above. Good black tea, 25 pounds. In that country you will find a cup of good, hot, black tea after a long, cold tramp, very invigorating — in fact, it proves "the cup that cheers but not inebriates." Coffee, 10 pounds; sugar (good granulated), 100 pounds. If you take the ordinary brown sugar in winter it freezes into a hard lump and is very difficult to manipulate. Not so with granulated; it remaining dry of course remains powdered. Beans, 120 pounds. There are several kinds of beans of which you may make choice according to your taste, but the ordinary bean sold here [in Edmonton and Vancouver] is the brown bean, about twice the size of the small white one. Pot barley, 10 pounds; rice, 15 pounds; extract of beef, two dozen four ounce tins. I have found Johnson's Fluid Beef to be very good. Baking powder, 12 to 15 pounds; salt, 30 pounds; pepper, one pound; mustard, one pound; compressed vegetables, 10 or 12 pounds, depending upon the kind you take. Canned fruit may or may not be taken, but they are bulky and heavy, consequently inconvenient and in winter a source of

trouble in that country, as the contents freeze solid and require a long time to thaw. You should also take 10 or 15 or more pounds of baking soda, as you may think necessary. In case of scurvy one might provide lime juice, more or less as their taste suggests, but the dried fruits already named are antiscorbutic in their action and if we wish to make further provision in that direction we might take two or three dozen tins of good orange marmalade, and similar quantity of strawberry or raspberry jam. These, as put up by some firms, are very good. Dried potatoes are put up in several forms and are good. 25 or 30 pounds of these should be taken. Other vegetables are put up also from which you may select as you fancy, but you should take the above quantity of potatoes or 8 or 10 pounds of dried onions. Take along also a few dozen yeast cakes; you may have a chance to use them once in a while, and their weight and cost are trifling.[7]

Though some other "experts" disagreed slightly about the amounts to be taken (McDougall and Secord's *Guide to the Gold Fields* suggested 400 pounds of flour and only 150 pounds of bacon), nearly all agreed with Ogilvie that the chief items in the provision list should be flour, bacon, beans, sugar and dried fruit. Many miners suffered severely, from both scurvy and malnutrition, for not paying careful attention to the advice offered by such experienced men as Ogilvie.

McAdam and his partners did not make that mistake. McAdam's own food-supply list included 300 pounds of flour, 175 pounds of bacon, 40 pounds of peas, 75 pounds of beans, 75 pounds of oatmeal, 40 pounds of rice, 40 pounds of dried apples, 40 pounds of prunes, 80 pounds of other dried fruits, 125 pounds of sugar and 80 cans of milk, in addition to the usual amounts of salt, baking powder and tea. And, like so many other Klondikers who anticipated a Christmas far away from home, he included a Christmas pudding. But even with this care, the provisions were, as we shall see, just sufficient to see him through his sixteen-month expedition.

Of next importance to being adequately fed was being adequately clothed. McAdam's list of personal supplies also gives ample evidence of the care with which he outfitted himself for his long trek and again William Ogilvie's advice was, by and large, the basis of the outfit:[8]

7. William Ogilvie, *The Klondike Official Guide*, pp. 137-138.
8. On page 139 of *The Klondike Official Guide* Ogilvie gives a complete list of the clothing and utensils needed, with the price for each that one would have paid in Edmonton.

1 sleeping bag	$25.00	1 pr. kneeboots	$4.50
2 pr. blankets	10.35	1 pr. rubber hip boots	4.60
1 fur-lined cap	1.75	1 pr. low rubber boots	.96
1 fur-lined coat	23.60	2 combs	.16
1 cordouroy coat,		1 soap box & soap	.34
vest and pants	19.00	1 tooth brush	.16
3 suits overalls	2.25	2 pr. buckskin mitts	.50
1 suit oilskins	3.00	2 pr. lined mitts	.40
4 suits winter under-		4 pr. dogskin gloves	1.50
clothes	9.00	2 pr. moccasins	2.00
1 doz. wool socks	2.50	½ doz. ties	1.40
1 pr. buckskin pants	15.00	1 Tam O'Shanter	.75
2 pr. cowhide pants	6.25	1 doz. handkerchiefs	.80
½ doz. towels	.82	2 pr. spectacles	.60
⅓ doz. towels	1.00	1 clothes bag	1.20
¼ doz. braces	2.10	1 pr. snowshoes	2.50
1 belt	.80	1 rubber sheet	3.00
2 felt hats	.50	1 rubber pillow	1.25
hatchet & pouch	.75	1 pack strap	3.00
1 sheath knife	.60	2 long straps	1.25
2 waterproof bags	1.75	1 leather comb & case	1.00
1 rifle	gift	stationery	2.00
rod and tackle	3.50	stamps	6.00
watch & chain	4.75		

William Ogilvie estimated that, at the very least, supplies for a single Klondiker for one year would cost $200. This proved to be a most conservative estimate; rarely could one get to the Klondike for that amount. McAdam's outfit alone cost him $214.07; in addition to this his commitment to the company which he and his five partners had formed cost another $552.12, the total cost of the expedition (including joint supplies, boats, rail and steamboat tickets, and other party expenses) being $2760.60.[9] Thus, the cost to Eben McAdam (and, we must assume, to each of his partners), at the very minimum, was $766.19 which, in 1898, was a sizeable sum of money. Was the risk, to say nothing of the hardship, worth it? Would the small sum pale into insignificance when the gold nuggets were weighed in? Or would there, after all the toil and trouble, be any gold at all to weigh in?

Those were some of the questions which Eben McAdam asked himself as he prepared for the most momentous journey of his life and they are the kind of questions which recur throughout

9. The figures are taken from McAdam's personal account book.

the diary which he kept during that journey. Indeed, it is this kind of questioning and soul searching which makes McAdam's diary of his journey to the Klondike the poignant and personal document that it is: it is a detailed description and personal commentary of an ordinary man performing an extraordinary feat of endurance.

For the most part, Eben McAdam's diary is a "day-to-day" account of the routine of travel — including tracking up northern rivers, crossing dangerous muskeg, setting up tents after a weary day's journey, making hurried meals, sleeping through forty-below nights, and packing and re-packing the more than 6,000 pounds of supplies. Thus, superficially, many of the entries may appear monotonous: "Up at 7 a.m. . . . Tracked till 7 p.m. Distance 3 miles!" But even these, when one imagines the toil involved (to make that mere three miles), are packed with frustration, weariness, doubt, and sometimes happiness.

The main interest of the diary, however, lies in those many long passages in which McAdam reveals what life was like during those long winter months when McAdam's party and almost fifty other miners were forced to camp on Wind River. The attempt to form some sort of government, the outbreaks of scurvy, the encounters with Indians, the entertainments and the never-ending longing to get over the mountain divide are vividly portrayed. It is these which give the diary its permanent value as an historical document and which make it eminently enjoyable.

The Diary of Eben McAdam

Thursday, March 17, 1898

Left Montreal at 2:45 on Wednesday, March 9, 1898; arrived at Duck Lake [Saskatchewan] on Saturday at 8:30 p.m. We occupied the smoking compartment of a colonist sleeping car together with an English Jew and another party of four bound for the Klondike.* The trip was pleasant, the Jew affording us much amusement. We stopped at McIntyre's Hotel at Duck Lake till Wednesday the 16th, 2 p.m. Owing to the teamster not meeting us on arrival, McG. [McGinnis] and McA. [McAdam] drove out to see that everything was alright. This little side trip used up the best part of Sunday and all day Monday. Our first experience in crossing country began on the afternoon of the 16th. Our intention on leaving was to make Carlton, 12 miles distant and camp for the night, but owing to the very heavy roads and [snow] drifts we made nine miles only and remained for the night. We succeeded in passing a fairly comfortable night under tent. Bob Isbister, his son, and man (we had three teams) sleeping around a campfire.** The experiences of the night taught us the necessity of making camp earlier in the day — at least one hour before sunset. Thursday morning we were up bright and early and crossed the Saskatchewan River about 12 o'clock. We reached Charlie LaFleur's at 2 o'clock and had dinner. We camped about 5:30 p.m. and used an outside tent and in consequence had a much more comfortable quarters than the night before when we used an inside tent.***

Editor's note: The first weeks of March, 1898, were very busy ones for those adventurers leaving Eastern Canada for the Klondike, the idea

9

being to reach the rivers as soon as the ice melted. Special trains were provided and the CPR and GRT doubled its contingent of cars to accommodate the goldseekers. The Montreal Gazette kept a running commentary on the Klondike activity, describing the parties arriving from Europe and the United States and heading for the Klondike.

**Bob Isbister, McAdam's teamster, probably belonged to the locally well-known half-breed family which had lived, hunted and guided in that area for a long time. When Milton and Cheadle (see The North-West Passage by Land, p. 113) passed through that area in 1865 an Isbister was their guide. James Isbister was one of the representatives (along with Gabriel Dumont and Michel Dumas) who, in June, 1885, persuaded Louis Riel to return from Montana and lead the Metis in their fight against the Canadian government's indifference to their demands and which resulted in the Riel Rebellion.

***What McAdam means, when he talks of an "outside" and "inside" tent, is that he used two tents for extra insulation, one inside the other. This apparently was not an uncommon practice.

Friday, March 18, 1898

Started about 7:30 a.m. and had dinner at Dr. Crowe's, Muskeg Lake and arrived at the Indian Agency about 8 o'clock.* Mr. Holton Krith, agent. We were Mr. Krith's guests till 10 o'clock next morning.

*Editor's note: The Indian Agency was situated on the Muskeg Lake Indian Reserve, 102.

Saturday, March 19, 1898

Started at 10 o'clock, arrived at Bob Isbister's about 3 o'clock where we had dinner, and reached Mr. Taylor's (Church of England Mission) about 8 o'clock.* Distance in the 3½ days about 60 miles. This morning, Sunday the 20th, we attended Service in the Mission Church. About 40 of the natives were present and were very attentive. The Squaws used the usual dress, the shawl and in several instances had their papooses with them. The Service was in the Cree tongue, and very pleasant to listen to. We attended again in the afternoon. Communion was observed in the morning.

*Editor's note: The mission seems to have been located at the southern end of the Atakakup Indian Reserve 104.

Monday, March 21, 1898

Today we mounted two of our sleighs. The other will be finished tomorrow. We will require three for freighting to the lakes. Bob is to provide five jumpers so that we will have eight loads all told.* Bob is also to provide the horses and shafts for our sleighs. The change from two horse rigs to the single was deemed advisable owing to the reported conditions of the roads. On our arrival at the Agency we learned that 21 jumpers had come in from Green Lake for the Hudson's Bay Company and had broken the road. Roads broken by jumpers, however, are not suitable for heavy teams (2 horses). In the evening we had a musical and retired about 12 o'clock.

*Editor's note: A "jumper" was a low, short sleigh set on heavy wooden runners, pulled either by dogs or a single horse.

Tuesday, March 22, 1898

This morning we arranged our small wares and articles not properly packed and emptied cases and in the evening finished our sleighs. During the afternoon I had a game of dominoes with Mr. Taylor. Our visit here is very pleasant. Mr. Taylor and his family are very kind people and are doing all they can to make us enjoy ourselves. It is quite amusing the manner in which the Indians will come into the house. Such a thing as knocking at the door and waiting to be let in is never done. They simply open the door and walk in. They are quiet and from what I could see they have few questions to ask but are always ready to answer any questions. As we are in the first party for the gold fields to pass this way, the natives are curious to see us, and quite a number have called. All have either French or English Christian names, but their surnames have Indian origins and usually come from some peculiar trait of character or superior ability in Indian arts.

Wednesday, March 23, 1898

We completed our sleighs and got everything ready. Bob Isbister and his men arrived about 11:30 a.m., but between making shafts for our sleighs and loading we could not leave before four o'clock. Our visit at the Mission was very pleasant and hospitable and although our stop there was much longer than we expected when leaving Duck Lake, we thoroughly enjoyed it and at the same time occupied ourselves with work that would have been necessary at Green Lake. We camped about 4 miles out, making camp about 6:30. A heavy snowstorm came up shortly before [we left] and kept up during the first part of the night.

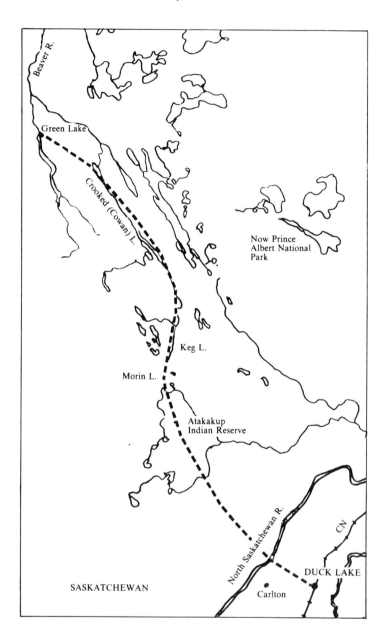

The first stage of Eben McAdam's journey: Duck Lake, March 12 to Green Lake, March 31

Thursday, March 24, 1898

Broke camp 7:45 a.m. and had dinner at a half-breed's house at the far end of Devil's [Morin?] Lake. Stopped 11:30 and left again at 1:30. When leaving the Indian said we would find the roads very heavy and did not think we would travel 2 miles. We did find the roads heavy but succeeded in making probably 4 or 5 miles. The walking was fatiguing and we were compelled to use our snow shoes the latter part of the afternoon. Camped at 5 o'clock and had our first meal of bacon, besides boiling a couple of pieces for lunch next day.

Friday, March 25, 1898

Thermometer registered 20° below at 5:30 a.m. (It registered 22° below the Sunday we spent at the Mission). Had a good hot breakfast including some warm boiled bacon. Broke camp at 8:30 and started immediately to cross Keg Lake. We were about two hours doing it and then entered the bush. While crossing Keg Lake the odour of sulphur was very noticeable. Springs rise here and there in the lake and all appeared to be strongly impregnated with sulphur. This lake is not considered very safe owing to the Springs weakening the ice in places. Had our mid-day meal in the woods, rested about an hour and a half. Camped about 5:00 p.m. Made probably 12 or 13 miles. Roads very heavy and had to use snow shoes.

Saturday, March 26, 1898

Thermometer at 5:30 about 15° below. Slept with my head well covered with the hood of [my sleeping] bag and in the morning found the breathing opening well covered with frost. Broke camp about 8:15 and travelled till about 10:30 when one of Bob's sleighs broke down. The delay caused a loss of three hours. Left at 1:30 and camped at 5:50 at the entrance to Crooked Lake [now Cowan Lake].

Sunday, March 27, 1898

Thermometer 28° below at 5:30 a.m. Broke camp at 8 o'clock. Roads on the lake were very heavy and we only made about 10 miles during the day. Camped 5:30. This lake resembles a river very much. It is only about ⅓ of a mile wide and stretches of about 7 to 10 miles can be seen at a time. This lake is also strongly impregnated with sulphur. We were compelled to travel Sunday as we were short of feed for the horses and had to make [for a place] where food could be had. Made about 10 miles.

Monday, March 28, 1898

Thermometer 20° below. Broke camp about 8:30 and camped again 6:30 making about 15 miles.

Tuesday, March 29, 1898

Thermometer 12° below. Broke camp at 7:45 and reached the end of the lake at 12:15 where we had dinner. Covered about 9 miles in the morning making the lake about 34 miles long.* In the afternoon the road led through the bush and some very bad muskeg. We made during the day about 18 miles. Camped 7:15.

*Editor's note: Cowan Lake is actually thirty miles long, so McAdam's calculations were not far out.

Wednesday, March 30, 1898

Thermometer 5° below. Broke camp at 7:30 a.m. and arrived at Green Lake at 11:30 and put up with Mr. Dreever, the H.B.C. Agent. On arriving here we were much surprised to learn that all arrangements had been made by Mr. King of La Crosse H.B.C. post to have us sent forward to Lac La Crosse and that the teams had been waiting our arrival for three or four days, and also that the price was to be $2.00 per hundred [weight]. It appears that Mr. King in an interview with Mr. Taylor a short time ago had mistaken a simple request for information as a contract and had acted accordingly.* We told Mr. Dreever that Mr. King had made a mistake as Mr. Taylor would not make such a contract without our authority and that not only did we not know of such a contract but had actually made an arrangement with Bob to freight us to Lac La Crosse. We told him, however, that owing to the bad condition of the roads we had just covered, Bob had decided not to go farther and that we were open to make an arrangement to go on but would not pay $2.00 per [cwt]. We finally agreed on a $1.50 rate, including some $19.00 expenses incurred by the men awaiting our arrival. We housed with Mr. Dreever during our stay here, three of us using our sleeping bags.

*Editor's note: According to notes found in the back of McAdam's diary, his share of the teamster's freighting costs was $37.75; it therefore cost the party nearly $200 to have their provisions freighted over those trails between Duck Lake and the Athabasca River.

Thursday, March 31, 1898

Left Green Lake at 3:30 p.m. with 12 single sleighs and 3 men. Crossed Green Lake and travelled a short distance on Crooked River [Cowan River] to near the Beaver River Junction. Camped 6:30. Distance 12 miles.

Friday, April 1, 1898

Thermometer zero. Broke camp 5:30 a.m. and travelled about 12 miles down Beaver River. Had dinner about 12 a.m. In the afternoon and evening we covered about 10 miles more. Camped at 9 p.m. Distance 25 miles.

Saturday, April 2, 1898

Broke camp at 4 a.m. and camped at 7:30 p.m. Distance 22 miles.

Sunday, April 3, 1898

Broke camp at 7:30 a.m. Had dinner about 11 a.m. and supper at 5:30. After supper continued travelling to 12:30 p.m. Crossed Big Bay Lake during the day. Distance 30 miles.

Monday, April 4, 1898

Broke camp at 10 a.m. and arrived at Isle a la Crosse at 12 a.m. Distance 6 miles. We were pleasantly received and hospitably entertained by Mr. and Mrs. King and Mr. Christie. Mr. King explained his interview with Mr. Taylor and said while he did not consider his interview with Mr. Taylor as a contract, he was desirous of helping any of Mr. T's friends as much as possible, and undertook to have matters arranged for us on our arrival at Green Lake. Arranged with Mr. K. for a through rate of $3.00 per hundred to Sulphur Springs [on the Clearwater River].*

Editor's note: One could hardly do better at this point than to read William Butler's excellent account of his journey along the same route and his description of the fort at Ile à la Crosse in 1873. See chapter eleven of The Wild North Land *(1873; rpt. by Hurtig, 1968). "It is not from its shape," states Butler, "that the lake takes its name; in the centre, where the four arms meet, stands an island, on the open shore of which the Indians in bygone times were wont to play their favorite game of la Crosse. The game named the island and the island in turn gave its name to the Lake" (p. 103).*

Tuesday, April 5, 1898

Spent the day at Isle a la Crosse and wrote several letters.

Wednesday, April 6, 1898

Left Isle à la Crosse at 8:20 a.m. with 13 single sleighs (3 our own) and 10 toboggans besides 4 loads of hay and fish for the dogs at Bull's House, at the head of Buffalo Lake — in all 17 loads and 7 men. Weight of supplies (less our sleighs) 6287 lbs. Camped at the head of La Crosse Lake at 6:30. Distance 20 miles.

Thursday, April 7, 1898

Broke camp at 6:45 a.m. Reached Deep River about 7:15 a.m. Had dinner at 10:30 a.m. Had some refreshment at short portage 3 p.m. (made to avoid dangerous ice). At this point Pierre Morin, one of the teamsters (the one who travelled with us from Green Lake to Isle a la Crosse) decided not to go any further as his horses were played out and the hay was not (he said) sufficient to see us through. After a lot of talk and waste of time he decided to go as far as the [Buffalo] Narrows. We continued our journey from 6:30 till about 8:30 and camped. Distance 18 miles.

Good Friday, April 8, 1898

Broke camp at 6:30 a.m. and reached the Narrows about 10:30 a.m. Yesterday's trouble had been brewing during the morning travel and on our arrival here Pierre again brought up the subject of not going farther. We said he could not go. As the rest of the men showed bad symptoms, we asked them how far they proposed going, and they said they were in the same predicament as Pierre. They finally decided not to go any further. Fortunately at this point the Hudson's Bay Company have two vacant buildings, so we told them if they did not want to go any further they had better place our supplies in one of the houses. They did so and left on their trip back to Isle à la Crosse about 1 p.m. During the unloading we had dinner and about 12 a.m. (one hour before the teamsters) McGinnis and Smith started back (45 miles) to see Mr. King and find out what was to be done. The rest of the day we remained quiet and had a good rest. Went to bed early.

Saturday, April 9, 1898

Had breakfast about 8 a.m. and after everything had been cleared away we set to work to repair the tent damaged by the sparks from our stove. This was quite a heavy job but we finally got through. We removed the tin pipe hold from the roof with the intention of replacing it at the door end, but finally decided not to make any place for the pipe at present. Retired early, in fact too early.

Sunday, April 10, 1898

Up early and had breakfast about 8 a.m. Passed the day quietly. During the morning Henry drew my attention to one of the Indians returning with a toboggan load of fish and we went over and had a look at them. The catch, the Indian said, was not a large one, that during the Summer months they make much larger hauls. Still, it struck us as a very good night's work. It consisted of whitefish, pike, dore, succors, catfish, and lush — all fish, with the exception of the whitefish, were familiar to us as residents of the old St. Lawrence. The pike were the largest we ever saw ranging from 6 to 12 pounds.

Monday, April 11, 1898

Still at the Narrows. Up at 6:15 a.m. and had breakfast — bacon, biscuits and tea. I removed the pipe hole from the remaining outside tent. McGinnis and Smith got back about 9 a.m. They left Isle a la Crosse at 7:30 the night before and travelled all night with dogs — covered 45 miles in 10½ hours. On Thursday night, the 7th, about 30 dog teams passed us on their way to Isle à la Crosse to spend Easter and this morning a large portion of them living at this point and beyond on this trail, arrived here. All stopped as the sun was high, those living beyond remaining till about 8:30 p.m. This is the first time I ever had a chance to see this method of travelling in operation and cannot say the impression was favorable. It was nothing but one continuous snarl or howl all day. It may be necessary to thrash the animals as the teamsters did in order to get the work out of them. Still, I am under the impression that a little more merciful handling of the whip would have answered just as well. When in harness the mere appearance of their masters was all that was necessary, even without the slightest motion to whip, for the poor animals to set up the most piteous howls. The dogs while travelling are fed 2½ fish a day, equal to perhaps 7 to 10 lbs. I paid particular attention to one team being fed. They were given one fish each and set to work immediately and in a very short time everything had disappeared. The fish, of course, are not cleaned. The Hudson's Bay Company's man from Buffalo Lake arrived with McGinnis and Smith this morning. McGinnis and Smith left for Bull's House at 6:00 p.m.

Tuesday, April 12, 1898

Still at the Narrows. Passed the day quietly. Nothing to do. Went to bed early.

Wednesday, April 13, 1898

Still at the Narrows. Passed the day very much like yesterday. The body of an Indian child was brought in for burial. We called (Charlie [Maltby] and myself) in the evening, and took over some tea and candles.

Thursday, April 14 and Friday, April 15, 1898

Still at the Narrows. Charlie and myself attended the funeral of the child. Fortunately for the poor people the priest was here from Isle à la Crosse, so they had a funeral service. Eight or nine men and women attended. We copied the custom of the people and each threw in a handful of earth. About 9:30 the dog teams began to arrive from Buffalo Lake [now called Peter Pond Lake]. At six o'clock I started with five dog teams (4 toboggans and 1 sled).* I crossed the portage, arriving there about 6:30 but had to wait till 8:45 before the first team put in an appearance, the last one coming in about 9:15. The portage is about ½ mile and the route the teams took (they could not cross the portage) about 7 miles. The men made a fire and had some tea, bannock and grease and three of them left about ten o'clock. One of the two remaining had to lighten his load for part of the way and after he had had his tea went back and brought on the pieces left behind. The last two teams left camp about 12 o'clock, and crossed the lower end of little Buffalo Lake and part of the second portage and camped again at 3 a.m. The road to this point was very bad, particularly the portage. On the lake we were in four or five inches of water most of the time and on the portage (or muskeg) still worse. We broke camp again at 4:30 a.m., finished the remainder of the portage and crossed a small lake and over the third portage about 50 to 100 yards into Buffalo Lake. One of the three who went ahead continued leaving the other two behind. We passed their camp about 5 a.m. but they caught up to us about 9 a.m. and we travelled together the rest of the day. Had tea about 3 times during the day resting about one and a half hours each time. The big lake road was in fairly good condition and continued so till night when we had about two hours of by far the worst tramping of the day, the water at several points reaching almost to the top of my knee boots. The knee boots proved a failure for such work. Of course mine were new, but under any condition moccasins, with wet feet would be a decided improvement. On my arrival at Bull's House found McGinnis up (he had been in bed) and he soon had a good pot of tea ready for the men and myself. At about 7 p.m. we passed six teams going to the Narrows to bring up the balance of the supplies.

Editor's note: McAdam, from what follows, did not drive a dog team himself, but merely left with that group of teamsters, allowing him, as he later states, to cross the portage, while the dog teams took a longer route.

Saturday, April 16, 1898

Had a fair night's rest and a good sleep in the middle of the day. Mr. McDiarmid [later referred to as McDermott] was in early. He is anxious to do all he can to push us through. The La Loche river at the rapids is open and he is arranging for supplies to go forward in canoes to the head of the river, where we take to the ice again.

Sunday, April 17, 1898

Three loads of supplies arrived today, but Maltby and Chomiere did not arrive although we expected them all day. Feel alright again but a little stiff.

Monday, April 18, 1898

Were waked up at 5:30 a.m. by the arrival of Maltby and Chomiere with the remainder of the supplies. They came by way of Buffalo River instead of Buffalo Lake, and remained a good part of the day at the river. We cannot move up La Loche river today; ice has to change.

Tuesday, April 19, 1898

Left Bull's House about 8:30 a.m. for a point about one mile up the river. The move is a short one, but always counts. We moved our goods with dogs. We put up [only one] tent as our

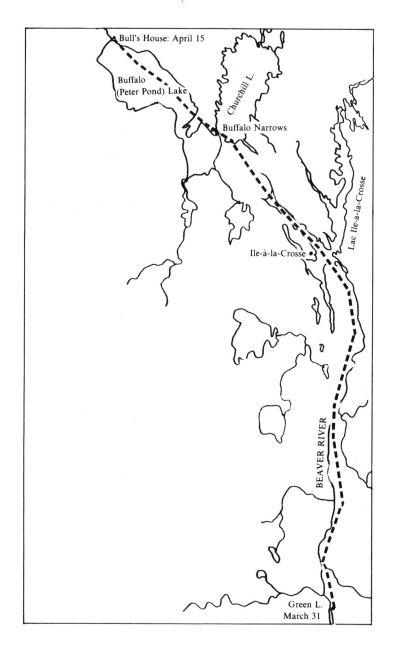

Bull's House: April 15

Buffalo
(Peter Pond) Lake

Churchill L.

Buffalo Narrows

Lac Ile-a-la-Crosse

Ile-à-la-Crosse

BEAVER RIVER

Green L.
March 31

McAdam's progress: March 31-April 15, 1898

stay at this place is indefinite. Henry's [Chomiere's] birthday and good wishes were in order.

Wednesday, April 20, 1898

Still at same point. Bark canoes arriving to be used at the very first opportunity. Rained lightly during the evening. We see wild ducks and geese every day now.

Thursday, April 21, 1898

Up at 6:30. Still at same point. Two more canoes arrived. Shortly after dinner began another short move up the river. Completed same in three trips and camped on fine high ground at 5:30 p.m.

Friday, April 22, 1898

Up at 6:30 a.m. McGinnis, Maltby and myself went up river a short distance and broke up the ice jam and cleared a very fair channel for the canoes, but when returning the ice shoved in shore and filled in the channel. Snow storms during the night.

Saturday, April 23, 1898

Still at same camp. Up at 7 a.m. Cannot move; river still jammed. Henry went out before breakfast and shot four mallard ducks. Miserable day — snow storm.

Sunday, April 24, 1898

Same camp. Up at 7 a.m. Sang hymns. McGinnis and Maltby read from the New Testament. Beautiful day. Robins seen for the first time.

Monday, April 25, 1898

Same camp. Up at 6 a.m. Cloudy. Ice shore at 12:30 a.m. This shore is apparently clearing the river. Moved camp a short distance up river to [be] clear of ice. Ice continued to run all day.

Tuesday, April 26, 1898

Up at 6:30 a.m. Ice all gone. Started up river with 10 canoes and 20 men. Cleared the lower rapids and camped at 6 p.m. We had some very heavy walking through willows along the banks, but probably the hardest work we have had as yet was crossing one or two portages through muskegs. Distance 12 miles.

Wednesday, April 27, 1898

Up at 4 a.m. Broke camp at 5:30 a.m. Each of us got into the canoes and those who could not get paddles, helped. Got out of canoes about three miles up and tramped to the head of the last rapid; had supper about 5:30 and all got into the canoes again and reached the lake [Lac la Loche] about 7:30 p.m. The tramping was even worse than yesterday's as it was mostly through muskeg. Wore my knee boots in the morning but found them so heavy, decided to wear my moose-top rubbers and in consequence found the walking less fatiguing. Feet soaking wet all afternoon and evening, and found the water very cold. (McDermott, H.B.Co., saw first rabbit this season.) Miserable camping place, so had to put up tent to shelter from North wind. Very little wood.

Thursday, April 28, 1898

Up at 6:30 a.m. Cannot move today. Most of the men left us, some for home and the rest to the head of the lake for teams. Two teams (dogs) left with loads of supplies.

Friday, April 29, 1898

Up at 4 a.m. Broke camp at 6 a.m. Crossed open water at foot of the lake in canoes and crossed the lake with dog teams (22). We stopped at the H.B. Co. post and had dinner with McDermott, most of the teams going on. Left post about one and reached the point where the supplies were at 2 p.m. When we left the post we understood that we would camp at the portage, but on making enquiries found that the portage was full one and a half miles distant, the reason given being that the ice was dangerous. This was all nonsense however, and simply an excuse for delay. Made camp and remained all night.

Saturday, April 30, 1898

Up at 6 a.m.; began teaming supplies across the upper end of the lake to the portage. Had to use canoes to land goods. In the afternoon moved goods to a point further inland — the sight of the old portage house — and camped at this place. We took supplies up in a canoe, a small river leading to the place.

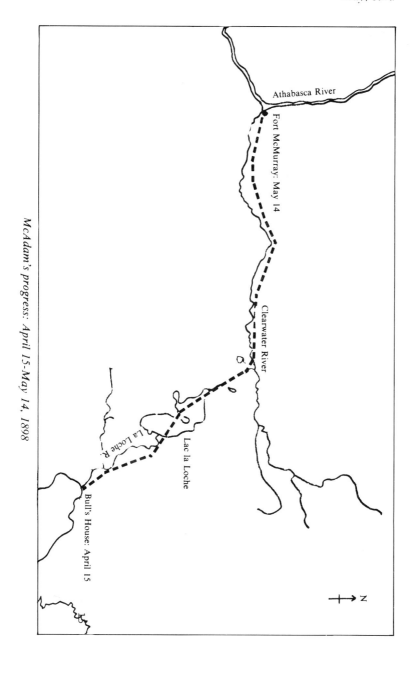

Athabasca River

Fort McMurray: May 14

Clearwater River

La Loche R.

Lac la Loche

Bull's House: April 15

McAdam's progress: April 15-May 14, 1898

N

Sunday, May 1, 1898

Rested all day. Weather beautiful and our camp in a beautiful place.

Monday, May 2, 1898

Up at 5 a.m. McDermott came up from the post at 9 a.m. and 7 pack horses arrived at 12 a.m. Plen McGinnis, Henry Chomiere and myself left at 2:30 p.m. for the Clearwater [River] and arrived there at 7:45 p.m.* Horses carried about 180 lbs. each. Roads in places were very bad, particularly down the slope of the mountain to the Clearwater River. The view from the top of the hill included quite a piece of the river and the mountains opposite and was very fine. There was a house at this end, also, when this route was used by the Company but only the ruins remain. It was not a post.

*Editor's note: It has taken McAdam and his party fifty-four days to reach the Clearwater River since leaving Montreal.

Tuesday, May 3, 1898

Up at 6:30 a.m. Men started back for another load about 8 a.m. and returned about 8 p.m. Tried to land a few fish but it was "no go" — not a bite.

Wednesday, May 4, 1898

Same camp and nothing to do. Went out in the morning and picked enough cranberries for two meals. Men did not start for the other side till 3 p.m. They evidently own the country and suit their work hours to their own convenience.

Thursday, May 5, 1898

Up at 6 a.m. Fine day. Mosquitoes beginning to be troublesome. McDermott arrived with packs about 7:30 p.m.

Friday, May 6, 1898

Up at 4:40. Plen McGinnis, myself and two Indians left with two canoes and supplies for the head of Terre Blanche rapids at 7:00 and arrived at 9:30. Distance about 15 miles. Men started back immediately after unloading. McGinnis and myself walked down to the rapids in the afternoon. They look bad. Magnificent view and for the hundredth time, regret not bringing a camera, if only for this end of the trip.

Saturday, May 7, 1898

Up at 6 a.m. McDermott and two Indians arrived at 10 a.m. with two loads. McGinnis and McDermott and Indian went down to view the rapids. All came back thoroughly satisfied that they are very dangerous. McDermott and Indians started back at 11 a.m. Began raining at 10:30 a.m. much to my disgust, as I was busily engaged doing some very necessary washing. Continued raining all day. Cleared about 8:30 p.m. Henry sent us a bear paw and McDermott gave us real duck; had a fricasee. Bear's paw a failure.

Sunday, May 8, 1898

Up at 6:30. Expected McDermott and Henry today, but they did not come. Miserable day, cold with snow flurries.

Monday, May 9, 1898

Up at 7:00, found weather cold, with tendency to clear.

Tuesday, May 10, 1898

Up at [undecipherable] a.m. Rest of the party arrived at 12 o'clock (noon) and after dinner, carried our goods in canoes down to the island at the head of Terre Blanche Rapids. After all the supplies had arrived at the island, we portaged across to the other side. We all gave a hand and I had my first experience carrying with the head strap. Carried over two loads, 80 and 100 lbs. Cannot say the experience was a pleasant one. The last load strained the muscles of the back of [my] neck, and the pain was so intense I thought I would have to throw the load down, but succeeded in landing the pack at the other side without a break. Distance about ¼ miles. After all goods had been carried over, we loaded canoes again and went down to the head of the next rapid and camped for the night.

Wednesday, May 11, 1898

Up at 6 a.m. Men took half loads down the rapids, balance was carried over portage. We again loaned [lent] a hand at carrying in order to save time. Today we had occasion to lighten the canoes three times for small rapids. The portages ranging from ½ to 1 mile. Camped about 6 p.m. at the head of a small portage.

Thursday, May 12, 1898

Up at 7 a.m. Men started with first load, before we were ready to move. Some taking canoes with small loads, the rest carrying. Left other side of portage at 12 a.m. and ran down to the head of Cascade Rapids. The portage for these rapids is 1½ miles long and the longest on the Clearwater. It was late in the afternoon before all was over, so camped for the night. When we began this last portage we understood Sulphur Springs were on farther side. During the afternoon, however, one of the men informed us that Sulphur Springs were several miles farther down and that we had more rapids to pass. McDermott said that he understood the contract to read the Sulphur's and that we were at the Sulphur's. Maltby, however, had a copy of the contract and it read Sulphur Springs, and showed it to McDermott who did not bring his papers with him. This settled the matter and arrangements were immediately made to properly complete the contract. This district for several miles is known as the Sulphurs, but the Springs proper occupy a small part only.

Friday, May 13, 1898

Up at 4 a.m. and had a light breakfast of biscuit and tea, and made an early start for the Springs. McDermott and three men accompanied us. We arrived at 8 a.m., passing only a few small shoals. We had our second breakfast here and at 10 a.m. McDermott and men started back. We were sorry to part with McDermott. He had been with us four weeks, and we always found him an agreeable companion and one desirous of helping us as much as possible. The men, however, we were glad to part with. Perhaps we should not form a bad opinion of these people as a whole, but so far as we had any direct connection with them we found them a grumbling, begging crowd. Immediately after McDermott's departure we embarked and began our journey without any assistance. Camped at 6:30 p.m. Had to pitch our tent on a miserable muskeg.

Saturday, May 14, 1898

Started at 7:30 a.m. Reached Pembina [Christina] River at 10 a.m. After a short run we reached the last rapid and ran it safely. Arrived at the branch of the Athabasca leading to Fort McMurray at 5 p.m. and the fort at 6 p.m. A few minutes after our arrival Mr. Flett in charge of the Hudson's Bay Co. post came down to see us and we learned that only four parties were ahead of us.*

Editor's note: For an enlightening and entertaining look at the Klondike parties which left Athabasca (via the "all-Canadian route") in the early months of 1898 see J. G. MacGregor's The Klondike Rush Through Edmonton (Toronto, 1970), particularly chapter seven.

Sunday, May 15, 1898

Up at 5 a.m. and remained in camp all day; did a few odds and ends in the way of preparing loads for the boats.*

Editor's note: McAdam and party had brought the four boats with them from Montreal, paying $67.00 for the boats and freighting to Duck Lake.

One of the "odds and ends" which McAdam attended to on May 15 was writing letters. This one, to his daughter Linda, survives:

> Fort McMurray
> 15th May 1898

> My dear little daughter —
> I sent a letter to you on the 13th inst. & it will be a race between that letter & this one & I would not be surprised if you get this one first. We are using boats now & we like the travelling much better. It is more pleasant & not such hard work. This is a very small place — only the Hudson's Bay Co's store & three or four houses & two Indian lodges. Tomorrow we begin to travel on the Athabasca River.
> Just as soon as you receive this letter I want you to write me a good long letter & address it to care
> Hudson's Bay Co.
> Fort Simpson
> Mackenzie River
> N.W. Ter.
> Canada
> I will write you again from Fort Chipewyan.
> I hope you are getting along well at school.
> With lots of love to Edith & yourself.

> Ever your affectionate father
> Eb McAdam

Monday, May 16, 1898

Left Fort McMurray at 10 a.m. and camped opposite Red River at 9 p.m. Distance 30 miles.

Tuesday, May 17, 1898

Up at 6:50 a.m. Camped at 7:30 p.m. Distance 30 miles.

Wednesday, May 18, 1898

Up at 4 a.m. and left at 5:20 a.m. Camped at [undecipherable]. Edith's [McAdam's elder daughter's] birthday. Distance 35 miles.

Thursday, May 19, 1898

Up at 2:30 a.m. and left camp at 3:30. Camped at 6 p.m. Distance 40 miles.

Friday, May 20, 1898

Up at 5:30 a.m. and left camp at 8 a.m. and reached Embarras River at 2:35 p.m. Had supper at 6 p.m. and then tarried an hour on shore and started again. Travelled several miles into the delta and camped at 9 p.m. Distance 28 miles.

Saturday, May 21, 1898

Left camp at 6 a.m. Reached Goose Island at 11:30. There was quite an Indian encampment there, and we stopped and made enquiries as to the direction to Fort Chipewyan. After a delay of about 20 minutes we started again to cross the lake. After about two hours row a breeze started up and freshened into a stiff blow and we took advantage of it and put up sails. We reached Chipewyan at 5:30. Maltby and Smith ran into an island opposite the post. We sent men over and they arrived in camp about 11 p.m.

$$\begin{array}{lr}\text{Distance to mouth of river} & \text{5 miles} \\ \text{Distance to Chipewyan} & \underline{12 \text{ miles}} \\ & 17 \text{ miles}\end{array}$$

Sunday, May 22, 1898

Up at 8:30 a.m. and went to church at 1:30. Mr. Lucas pastor. The church was well filled, and the whole service was in English. We enjoyed it very much. When coming in yesterday McGinnis stuck on a sand bar half a mile from shore, and Mr. Lucas, seeing the boat in trouble, went out in his own boat, took off part of the load and took it ashore. In the evening we attended a musical service in the school house conducted by Mr. Lucas. During the day Dr. MacKay, in charge of the H.B.Co. post, was very attentive to our needs and sent us down a jug of milk and three Waries [sic.]. We called on him in the afternoon to talk over the next part of our trip. He gave us a map of the route to

Fort Smith, but advised us to take a guide. Before coming away we needed to complete arrangements here for a guide and also for the portage at Fort Smith,* the Dr. promising us that we would be the first to cross the portage — the first by this route — a report having come in that a number of barges had come down the Peace River.** If this was true they would reach the portage first, and probably would be using the teams when we got there. If so, we might be delayed a day or so but not otherwise.

Editor's note: The portage referred to here is the sixteen mile portage from Smith's Landing (now Fitzgerald) to Fort Smith. "Over this," writes J. G. McGregor, "everything had to be hauled, and the long string of ox-drawn Red River carts, which had been adequate for the regular northern trade, was (in the summer of 1898) hopelessly overtaxed. The previous year the rate per hundred pounds for this service had been fifty cents, but the demand created by the competitive Klondikers had pushed it up to $1.50."

**Instead of taking the Edmonton-Athabasca Landing-Athabasca River route or the route taken by McAdam, almost a hundred Klondikers took the Peace River route. Either they travelled overland to Fort St. John or made their devious way from Athabasca Landing to Fort St. John; from that point they proceeded down the Peace River to the Slave River, where they joined the other Klondikers who had come by the more usual routes. See McGregor, The Klondike Rush Through Edmonton.*

Monday, May 23, 1898

Were waked up at 4:30 a.m. by Dr. MacKay calling to us to look after our boats as the sea was running high, the boats rubbing. We turned out without delay and fixed the boats. The storm continued all day and we were compelled to remain on shore.

Tuesday, May 24, 1898

Up at 5 a.m. Broke camp and started down river at 9:30 a.m. Camped at Des Roches River [now Riviere des Rochers] at 6 p.m. Day was very disagreeable; a stiff breeze prevailed most of the day with a heavy rain in the afternoon and evening. We were much disappointed to learn from our guide, Tom, that we would have to row up current to the junction of the Peace River. When the Peace River is high it reverses the current, and it runs into Lake Athabasca instead of out of it.* In the evening we sang "God Save the Queen" and "Rule Brittania." Distance about 9 miles.

Editor's note: E. J. Corp, who travelled this route a little later, elaborates on McAdam's statement: "The country between Lake Athabasca and the mouth of the Peace River is practically flat, so that in spring the waters of the Peace River coming from the south are in flood before the lake has risen, causing the slow running La Loche River to reverse its flow and go back into the lake for a day or two." (The Arctic Circular, *IX [1959], 35-51). Corp goes on to tell the story of some bewildered Klondikers who, having camped before the reverse flow started, awoke, started out, thought they were going upstream, and had to go ashore again. A passing crew explained the situation and saved them endless argument and embarrassment.*

Wednesday, May 25, 1898

Up at 5:30 a.m. Heavy head wind. Cannot leave camp this morning. Left camp at 3 p.m. and travelled till about 8 p.m. Distance 8 miles.

Thursday, May 26, 1898

Up at 6 a.m. Very windy; started at 10 a.m., passed the mouth of Peace River at 5 p.m. and began rowing down current. Stopped at 6 p.m. for supper, continued on our way at 7 p.m. and camped at 10 p.m. Distance 20 miles.

Friday, May 27, 1898

Up at 4 a.m. Broke camp at 6 a.m. Worked hard all day with the intention if possible of arriving at Smith's Landing tonight. We succeeded in doing so about 9 p.m. My hands were very sore and did a little sailing. Mosquitoes very bad and had to wear netting during the last hour's work in the water. Distance 47 miles.

Saturday, May 28, 1898

Did not get to bed till 2 a.m. We worked till all supplies were under canvas and boats on land. Up at 8 a.m. McGinnis left at 9 a.m. for Fort Smith to see Mr. McKinley and make arrangements for portaging our goods. Visited various camps. About 15 parties here.* Appear to be a nice lot of fellows. Mosquitoes a regular plague.

Editor's note: McAdam will, from time to time, mention the names of those other Klondikers; for a list of the parties which left Edmonton in the spring of 1898 see MacGregor, pp. 260-262.

Sunday, May 29, 1898

Up late. Still at Smith's Landing. Nothing to do. McGinnis did not return.

Eben McAdam, circa 1925

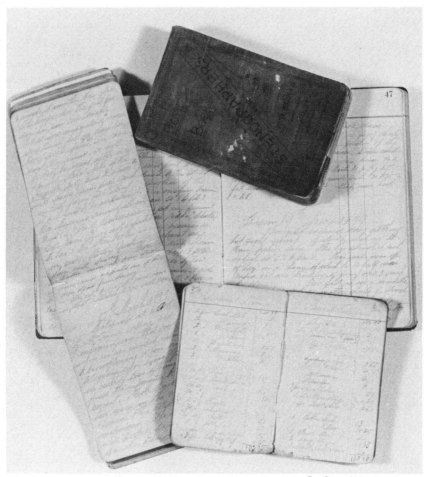

Eben McAdam's diaries

The McAdam party at Fort Chipewyan, late May, 1898. Eben McAdam is second from left.

Studio picture of Klondikers: Mitchell, Campbell and Fraser group.

The Hudson's Bay Company's steamer, "Wrigley," took the McAdam party part of the way to the Klondike.

"Wrigley" photographed at the junction of the Mackenzie and Liard rivers, 1200 miles north of Edmonton.

Pictured is a typical Klondike boat and crew which travelled with McAdam's party.

Klondikers are photographed building boats on the Athabasca River.

The Clark party is leaving Athabasca Landing in the spring of 1898. These boats are typical of those used by the parties mentioned in McAdam's diary.

"Off for the Klondike." The boat, "Jesse," is shown in full sail on the Athabasca River, 1898.

As indicated in the text, not all Klondikers travelled by the water routes. Here are two photos showing Klondikers going overland: the first by horse and sleigh, the second by the novel, but unsuccessful means of horse and barrel.

Monday, May 30, 1898

Continue to live at Smith's Landing. Nothing to do. McGinnis returned today. Several parties here before us have contracts on hand with the Hudson's Bay Co., but McKinley promised to see us through without any unnecessary delay.

Tuesday, May 31, 1898

Smith portage still and nothing to do. Today we decided to take the steamer at Fort Smith for Fort Providence.* This will necessitate a long wait, but considering the risk of crossing Slave Lake and the chance of delay there we think it best to take the steamer. Cold but bright.

*Editor's note: The "steamer" was the "Wrigley," a ninety-foot, propellor-driven boat which plied the waters of Great Slave Lake, the Mackenzie River and Great Slave River as far as Fort Smith. McAdam later refers to her as "new", but she was built in 1887. See William Ogilvie's The Klondike Official Guide, *p. 102, for a description of the "Wrigley," how she was built and the route she navigated.*

Wednesday, June 1, 1898

The stay at the Landing is becoming monotonous, but must be put up with. We are waiting patiently our turn to be portaged. In the evening we attended a concert (guitar and harmonica) in the Springfield, Illinois camp. Pleasant lot of fellows and had a good time.

Thursday, June 2, 1898

Today 29 boats arrived. This is the largest number to arrive in one day. All came from Athabasca Landing. Anderson of Montreal arrived with his partner, nine men in three boats: "Rose," "Shamrock" and "Thistle." The Anderson party and eleven other boats left to run the rapids after a rest of a couple of hours.* There are quite a number of rapids to run — three have to be portaged. Attended another concert in the Springfield camp and enjoyed it.

*Editor's note: Very few Klondikers ran these rapids for, as Ogilvie points out, between Smith's Landing and Fort Smith they aggregated a fall of 240 feet. Those who did attempt it on their own, like Cresswell's party, did so by trekking the boats and portaging around several of the worst rapids. It could take almost two weeks to do it. See R.H.S. Cresswell, "Overland Trail to the Klondike," Alaska Sportsman, *29 (May 1963), p. 20. Others, like George Mitchell, had the contents of their boats portaged and they accompanied the empty boats to Fort Smith. See Angus*

Graham, The Golden Grindstone: The Adventures of George M. Mitchell, *pp. 59-61.*

Friday, June 3, 1898

Passed day quietly. Teams returned from Fort Smith, and Alex (H.B. Co. man) promised to give us two to begin our work tomorrow. Henry and myself to go. Loaded one cart with boats.

Saturday, June 4, 1898

Up at 4:30, breakfast at six. Alex says he can only let us have one cart, so we left the boats behind and made a load of our sleeping bags and grub. Did not start till 10:30 and camped for dinner about 3 p.m. Arrived at Fort Smith at 8:30. Distance 18 miles. Road for two thirds the distance was very good; balance was muskeg and mud. It was 12 p.m. before we got to bed. Jack Grose's tent is within a few feet of ours.*

Editor's note: Jack Grose belonged to a large party of Klondikers who had originally intended to take the overland route. At Peace River Crossing, however, many of them had had enough of that route and about half the party, including Grose, went down the Peace River to the Great Slave River.

Sunday, June 5, 1898

Henry and I are alone and not much to do. Went down to the landing and on board the new H.B. Co. steamer. There are quite a few boats through to this point and most of them are remaining, awaiting reports about the ice. Mosquitoes are very bad and smudging does not appear to bother them. Very warm.

Monday, June 6, 1898

Carts returned to upper landing today, but do not expect rest of party till tomorrow. Mosquitoes worry us badly.

Tuesday, June 7, 1898

Up late and had only two meals today. Expect next party about 8 p.m. This is a miserable place and one of the poorest H.B. Co. posts we have seen. Back a few miles from here the Wood Buffalo are to be seen, although seldom at this time of year. The law protects them till 1900, but it is thought probable

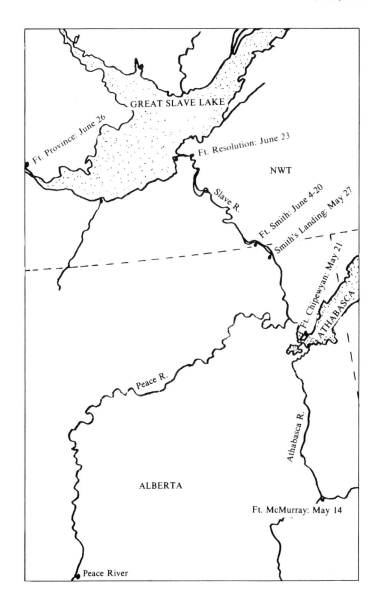

GREAT SLAVE LAKE

Ft. Province: June 26

Ft. Resolution: June 23

NWT

Slave R.

Ft. Smith: June 4-20

Smith's Landing: May 27

Ft. Chipewyan: May 21

ATHABASCA

Peace R.

Athabasca R.

ALBERTA

Ft. McMurray: May 14

Peace River

McAdam's progress: May 14-June 26, 1898

that the time will be extended.* An Indian living here shot one this Spring. He was fined $25.00 and the carcase taken from him. McGinnis, Maltby and Tom arrived about 8 p.m.

Editor's note: McAdam is here referring to the law passed in 1877 by the government of the NWT for the protection of the wood buffalo. See F. G. Roe's definitive study of the subject, The North American Buffalo *(Toronto, 1951).*

Wednesday June 8, 1898

Nothing to do so I borrowed a novel from Capt. Mills' wife ("The Demoniac" by Walter Besant) and spent most of the day reading. Sun set at 10:30 p.m.

Thursday, June 9, 1898

Very dull; cannot get reliable reports from the lake (Great Slave) or whether the steamer "Grahame" has arrived at upper landing.* Capt. Mills cannot say when we will leave, and everything is indefinite. This evening a guide was knocked out of a boat by sweep [by the sweep of an overhanging branch] and managed to get on to an island out in the rapids. Four Indians offered to go and get him for $20.00 each. Capt. Mills went out and brought him ashore.

Editor's note: The "Grahame" was on the Athabasca River, carrying Klondikers from Fort McMurray to Smith's Landing. It was probably for a full load that the Captain of the "Wrigley" was waiting.

Friday, June 10, 1898

Up late. What is the use of getting up early? Did a little darning that was necessary and read part of the novel "Beatrice" by Rider Haggard. Callers continually coming in.

Saturday, June 11, 1898

Up late about 9 a.m. and had breakfast at 10 a.m. After breakfast Henry and myself went down to the river and I washed all my soiled clothes. The river is quite a long way distant and down a steep standy bank and we found it much less work to do washing there.

Sunday, June 12, 1898

Up late. Nothing to do.

Monday, June 13, 1898

Same as yesterday.

Tuesday, June 14, 1898

Up late; breakfast at 9 a.m. Decided to improve my head rest during sleeping hours, so I bought some material from Mr. McKinley (H.B. Co.) and made a pillow and slip. Could not get feathers, but expect to get them at [Fort] Resolution or Providence. Jack Grose bought one of the "unknown" fish (Mackenzie River salmon) and sent it to us. In return we invited him to a dinner of baked fish and potatoes. This fish is fine eating.

Wednesday, June 15, 1898

Up about 8; breakfast 9 a.m. New steamer went out for trial trip today. She went out without ballast and there was considerable vibration. Screw was 8 inches out of the water. Cold all day.

Thursday, June 16, 1898

Day considerably warmer and as a consequence mosquitoes very bad. McKinley and Grose came to dinner and we had a fine spread. Baked fish and potatoes, bacon and lambsquarters (greens).

Friday, June 17, 1898

Up at 8:30; breakfast at 9 a.m. Heavy rain in the morning and very warm in the afternoon. Mosquitoes bad. Mrs. Mills (Capt. Mills' wife) took dinner and supper with us. They are breaking up housekeeping here preparatory to moving to Fort Simpson and their cook is on board the steamer.

Saturday, June 18, 1898

Passed a miserable night; cheered up with mosquitoes. The Captain says we will probably move out on Monday.*

Editor's note: McAdam seems to be feeling the effects of boredom at this point. Other Klondikers, it seems, did not find Fort Smith quite as boring as McAdam. George Mitchell, for example, spent most of his time getting into and breaking up fights. Here is how his first introduction to Fort Smith is described: "Fort Smith was a substantial log post, with a big parade-ground in front of the main building, log cabins for visitors and bettermost Indians, and space for a large number of teepees. As Mitchell came in at the gate he was amazed to see a squaw, wearing pink silk corsets outside her other clothes and a pair of high-heeled shoes, strolling about the parade-ground. It appeared that she lived in one of the huts, and was a more or less acknowledged institution — the priest said that she always showed her mettle in this way when strangers arrived. Mitchell was kindly received by the Company's people, and secured the loan of a heavy block and tackle for the next day. He spent the night in one of the cabins after having successfully resisted a warm invitation (not from the pink corsets) to spend it elsewhere." (Graham, The Golden Grindstone, *p. 62).*

Sunday, June 19, 1898

Up at 8:30. Cloudy day with slight rain. Springfield, Illinois fellows came up in the evening and brought guitar and we had a sacred song concert.

Monday, June 20, 1898

Up at 7 a.m. Expect to move out today if the weather improves. Passed a miserable night. Heavy gale all night and the rain came through the tent. Capt. Mills about 10 a.m. told us to get on board immediately after dinner. All on board at 3 p.m. and the steamer started about 5 p.m. with eight barges in tow.

Tuesday, June 21, 1898

Sailed all night and stopped for 4 hours early next morning to take on wood. Breakfast 7 to 9 a.m., dinner at 12. Supper at 6 p.m. Meals are very plain but the cooking is good. The baked beans are the best I have ever tasted. The Great Slave River below Fort Smith contained the same as above, low banks and a great many islands. At times the scenery is beautiful. Strong wind all day, with rain and we laid to early in the evening for the night.

Wednesday, June 22, 1898

Steamer started at 8:45 a.m. and dropped anchor at 1 p.m., where we remained the balance of the day. We are close to the lake but three buoys have to be set and they cannot be taken out in the jolly boats owing to the heavy sea.* In the evening the Springfield boys came aboard and we had some music. Passed the Cowan party today about 60 miles from [Fort] Resolution.

*Editor's note: The Slave River at this point runs through flat alluvial country and is quite silted in some places. Obviously it was the responsibility of Captain Mills to place buoys to mark the shallow spots.

Thursday, June 23, 1898

Remained at same anchorage till 4 a.m., when we started out (left barges behind) to set the buoys. Returned for barges about 8 a.m. and started again for Resolution where we arrived at 11 a.m. Resolution is a small place, but has the most imposing church edifice (RC) that we have seen in the country.* The fort is also one of the best. We expected to see a great many boats here, perhaps 30 or 40, but found only 15; all had gone ahead. The lake, we were informed, has been clear of ice since May 28th and all the various reports which we heard at Chipewyan proved mostly lies. We left Resolution at 8:45 p.m. with 10 new barges in tow. We go to an island 4 miles out for wood and to pick up the 8 barges we brought from Fort Smith.

*Editor's note: Fort Resolution was not, by northern standards, such a small place. McGregor describes it this way: "Fort Resolution . . . was an important point where C. F. Gaudet, a member of a highly respected northern family, was in charge of the Hudson's Bay Company's post. . . . Between the traders and their families and a few native families who lived there most of the time, Fort Resolution had a population of 108. In summer, however, some six hundred Indians who lived in the tributary area came in to trade." (MacGregor, Klondike, *p. 13).*

Friday, June 24, 1898

Left Wood Island off Resolution with 18 barges at 9:30 a.m. Beautiful day with good stiff breeze.

Saturday, June 25, 1898

Arrived at Hay River at 2 a.m. We called in at this place for wood and to leave mail. I was on deck when we arrived and went on shore. Met Mr. Marsh, the Church of England missionary and was invited up to the house; was introduced to Mrs. Marsh and Miss Marsh (Mr. M's sister) and two other ladies. Four white women in one settlement is a very unusual number in this part of the world. Had refreshments and Fred Dench gave us some music. Left Hay River at 8 a.m. and arrived at the mouth of the Mackenzie at 4 p.m. This part is full of islands and some distance farther it opens out into a wide gulf that resembles a lake. We arrived at the River proper about 12 p.m. Beautiful day, very little wind. Sun sets at 10 p.m. But it is quite light all night.

Sunday, June 26, 1898

Was waked up at 2 a.m. by the steamer running aground. Did not get up till breakfast time. Barges all gone drifting down to

[Fort] Providence. After breakfast we shifted part of the cargo to the forward hold, and carried out the anchor to a distance of 100 to 150 feet and drew the boat off with the windlass. The men on the barges were asked to send a pilot, John Hope, up from Providence, 8 miles. The pilot arrived at 1:30. We arrived at Providence at 3:30 and left again at 4:00. Stopped at Wood Island at 5:30 and left again at 6:30 p.m. We did a little fishing while the steamer was taking on wood. Caught 6 blue fish (was told by Mr. Booth, a passenger, that this fish is the English Grayling). We saw thousands of black ducks. Beautiful evening.

Monday, June 27, 1898

Another fine day and progress good, considering the heavy tow [i.e. the number of barges being towed]. Expect to arrive at [Fort] Simpson by supper time. Arrived at Fort Simpson at 7:30. Capt. Mills says we may remain on board the steamer. Fort Simpson commands a fine view of the river and the junction of the Liard River. A flight of 65 steps, cut in the clay bank leads from the shore up to the high land where the fort is situated. We are travelling together with the Springfield-Illinois party: Dick Feltham, Fred Dench, Doc. Waterman, Chas. Conklin, Chas. Vogelsand, Jack Grover, Dave Mulholland, Fred Payzant and Ralph Crichton of Halifax.*

Editor's note: There is a slight confusion here, for not all belonged to the Springfield-Illinois party; several parties were represented, some of whom later split up to form new parties.

Tuesday, June 28, 1898

Had breakfast on board the steamer. Purchased for $40.00 a large York boat from a party returning and intend to cover the balance of the Mackenzie River in it and enjoy a great deal more comfort. In the afternoon we brought the York boat down to the steamer and loaded it. Bought quite a number of things from same party including 500 lbs. of flour at $15.00 per cwt and a retort [glass cooking container]. Arranged to go down to Gravel River [now Keele River] with the Springfield-Illinois party and the two boys from Halifax.

Wednesday, June 29, 1898

Slept on board the steamer and had breakfast and dinner on board. Left Fort Simpson at 2:30 p.m. Caught up to Springfield about 6 p.m. Grose, with two Indians and the Halifax boys, caught up later. Floated down stream together all night. Had music in the evening.

Thursday, June 30, 1898

Arrived at Nahani River at 2:30 and found four boats there. Did not stop long. Separated from the Springfield in the morning and did not couple up again till evening. Put in to shore at 11 p.m. owing to a heavy rain storm and remained there till 1:30 a.m. Mosquitoes very bad all night.

Friday, July 1, 1898

Dominion Day. Passed [Fort] Wrigley at 11:30 a.m. Did not stop as landing is very poor. Jack Grose caught up to us at 1 p.m. and remained with us all day and night. Reached Blackwater River at 11 p.m. and anchored till morning.

Saturday, July 2, 1898

Charlie McGinnis, Henry and myself and Dick Feltham, Dave Dench and Dave Mulholland went up the Blackwater to prospect and returned about 12 a.m. I panned out a couple of times and saw colours for the first time. River very bad to go up and we decided not to try it. Left for the Gravel River at 1:30 p.m. and arrived at 11 p.m. Anchored for the night.

Sunday, July 3, 1898

Three or four parties here (Gravel River). Several men tried to go up yesterday; they report the river very difficult and say they met an Indian who told them they could not go up; that we should go down to [Fort] Norman, procure guides and cross the country 30 miles to a point 60 miles from the mouth of the Gravel River. Left Gravel River at 12 a.m. and arrived at Fort Norman at 11 p.m. Before going to bed I took a walk and met Rev. Mr. Spendlove, cousin of Dr. Spendlove of Montreal. During our conversation he said that from what he knew of the country he thought crossing the country with guides and a few provisions quite practicable, and he understood we could go to the headwaters of the McMillan in about 20 days. The great difficulty would be to get our supplies over. Thought this would be a very difficult matter to arrange.*

Editor's note: It is clear that McAdam, like so many other Klondikers, was very vague about the routes they should take. They were depending, to a very great extent, on the information provided by the

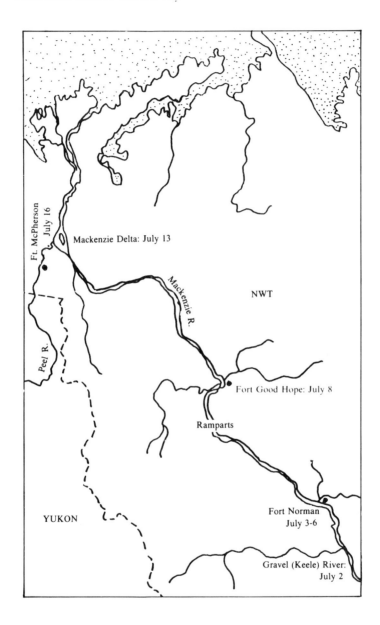

Ft. McPherson
July 16

Mackenzie Delta: July 13

Peel R.

Mackenzie R.

NWT

Fort Good Hope: July 8

Ramparts

YUKON

Fort Norman
July 3-6

Gravel (Keele) River:
July 2

McAdam's progress: July 2-July 16, 1898

natives and Hudson's Bay men, all of whom had different opinions about the best route. Thus the reason for McAdam's change in plan, ignoring the Gravel for the Peel. Maps, such as the one provided by Ogilvie, were very poor.

Monday, July 4, 1898

Heavy storm began early this morning and we cannot put out. We had to shift our boat down to the mouth of the Bear River. In the afternoon considerable quantities of ice came down and we rowed across to the opposite side of Bear River. Decided we would start for Peel River soon as the storm is over.

Tuesday, July 5, 1898

Storm still continues and we cannot move. Cold, but no mosquitoes.

Wednesday, July 6, 1898

Left [Fort] Norman at 8:30 p.m. Just before leaving we saw the Great Bear Lake Indians come in for their annual Summer visit. They were a miserable lot of creatures and did not appear to have many skins with them. They kept up a continuous fusilade as they neared the Fort.

Thursday, July 7, 1898

A warm day with very little wind and we are making good time drifting. Passed a lot of ice on shores.

Friday, July 8, 1898

Very little wind during the night and we travelled well. Passed the Sans Sault Rapids at 8 a.m. Entered Ramparts at 8:45 p.m.* The scenery here is beautiful. The river runs between two walls of yellow sandstone, ranging from 100 to 200 feet high. The length of the Rampart is about 8 miles. Arrived at Good Hope at 11 p.m. Went ashore and found most of the natives moving. Post looked beautiful in the distance, but a closer view proved disappointing. Young Mr. Gaudet, son of the H.B. Co. agent, was up. Procured two pairs of moccasins and a pair of slippers.

*Editor's note: The Ramparts is a deep gorge in the river, the depth of the water reaching fifty fathoms. For a description of this part of the river (and indeed the whole river) see Ogilvie's The Klondike Official Guide, pp. 100-108.

Saturday, July 9, 1898

Left Good Hope at 12:30 a.m. My watch and I did not get to bed till 5:30 a.m. During the watch the weather was good and we made good time. During the night we crossed the Arctic Circle. Shortly after going to bed a head wind set in and we did not cover more than 50 miles. From 12 p.m. till 2 a.m. a magnificent rainbow occupied the sky. We are hoping to see the midnight sun.

Sunday, July 10, 1898

Head wind all day. A heavy storm set in at 3 a.m. and we put ashore where we remained till 1 a.m. We utilized the time sleeping. Another slow day for travelling. We travelled part of the time with the Huron and "We're Here" parties.

Monday, July 11, 1898

Head winds all day. We ran part of the day coupled with Springfield, Huron, "We're Here" and Halifax. We had to separate at 5 p.m. owing to the storm. Another poor day for travelling. Cannot agree as to where we are. Maps do not show any prominent points that we can identify our position by.

Tuesday, July 12, 1898

Head winds still continue. In the afternoon the five boats had to separate again. We went ashore about 8:30 p.m. "We're Here" and Huron passed us between 9 and 10 p.m. Springfield came up at 11:30 p.m. and we coupled again and floated all night with "We're Here," Huron, Springfield, Halifax and Hetu and Millet [two Klondikers on their own].

Wednesday, July 13, 1898

On watch till 5 a.m. Passed Red River at 4:30 a.m. Hetu and Millet parted at 4 a.m. to call at Red River; the rest went on. Slept till noon and when we got up we found we had made a serious mistake. Instead of keeping to the left shore to strike into the Peel River, we had run into the Mackenzie River Delta. We started back for the head of the Delta at 5:30 and got into the right stream at 1:30 a.m. Had our first experience at tracking [walking the banks and towing the boat], and did not find it very hard work although part was along the top of a bluff and the trees interfered a good deal with the lane.* Coupled up once more with the Springfield, Huron and Halifax at 1 a.m. [perhaps should be 2 a.m.] and floated down to the Peel River which we reached at 3 a.m. Small stern wheeler with one barge passed us at 5 a.m. and the pilot told us we were on the right river. During the night we had the great satisfaction of seeing the midnight sun. We were so placed that we had the Mackenzie River for a horizon and consequently nothing to interfere with our view. At lowest dip only half the sun disappeared. This position was maintained from 11:30 p.m. till 12:30 a.m.

Editor's note: "Tracking" was, as all Klondikers attested, the most gruelling task. Here is how George Mitchell described it:

> *Our tracking line was a hundred and fifty feet long and about as thick as your middle finger. It was the kind of line that is made specially for the Hudson's Bay Company in the North of Ireland — pure flax, and quite unbreakable. You attach the line to the bow of the boat with a bridle, on the side away from the shore, extend it to its full length, and space the crew out along it as desired. Each man has a canvas sling which he attaches to the line with a knot that can be undone, and he slips his head and one arm through this and pulls with the sling over his shoulder. The sling must always be loose, so that you can duck out of it quick, because if the steersman makes the slightest mistake the boat may take charge and sweep the whole bloody crew off the cliff into the river. You have to make your way wherever there happens to be footing along the bank, and if there is thick bush you send the two best axemen ahead to clear a path. And when you are going in the water you mustn't go deeper than the crotch, for then the water begins to float your weight and you lose all power for pulling. After you've got the boys all out along the line and stepping her along nicely, perhaps the channel switches over to the opposite bank; and then you have to get them across the river and start all over again. No, I can tell you we miners found tracking the last damn thing on God's earth. (Graham, The Golden Grindstone, pp. 87-88).*

Thursday, July 14, 1898

Left at 2 p.m. to go up the Peel River. Tracked till 9:30 p.m. Banks were very good and we did not find the work very hard. Mosquitoes very bad and we anchored in mid-stream for the night. We saw our first view of the Huskies [Eskimoes] shortly after anchoring. Two boats passed.

Friday, July 15, 1898

Began tracking at 9:30 a.m. and at 8 p.m. put into the mouth of the branch leading to Rat River. Found several parties here, most of them busily engaged in reducing the size of their boats and building small boats for work in the portage of the Porcupine. We remained all night.

Saturday, July 16, 1898

Favorable wind began early in the morning and the Huron sailed out early. Springfield, Halifax and ourselves started out at 9 a.m. and made the run of 12 miles in six hours, reaching [Fort] McPherson at 3 p.m. About 12 boats here.*

*Editor's note: "After mid-summer, 1898, and throughout the following winter," writes J. G. MacGregor, "Fort McPherson was the busiest spot north of Edmonton. In 1898 . . . some five hundred Klondikers descended on the post." (MacGregor, Klondike, p. 150).

Sunday, July 17, 1898

Remained in camp; the rest went to church. The Huskies are here for the summer. A camp of about 12 lodges are here at present. The miners first to arrive have spoiled them by giving extravagant prices for everything they got from them. I secured a pipe, a pair of hip buttons [perhaps this should be "boots"?] and two hooks.

Monday, July 18, 1898

Still at Fort McPherson. Fred Dench, Dick Feltham and "Doc" Waterman have separated from the Springfield party and purchased the "We're Here" and are going up the Peel River as a separate party. Huron party are making their boat lower to have less draught. When these parties are ready we will start together.

Tuesday, July 19, 1898

Got a map of the river today from a miner who received particulars from the only Indian who has been over the watershed portage [the divide between the Peel and the Stewart Rivers; the Stewart leading to Dawson City]. We hope it is reliable. We cannot gain any information and do not get any encouragement from people here. Only one guide here and he is engaged, and claims there is an easy portage over to a river running into the Yukon. Is it the Stewart? Other parties are about ready and we expect to make a break tomorrow early. Caught a couple of dozen dace off the boat. Ran about half to three-quarter pounds. Sweet but full of bones.

Wednesday, July 20, 1898

Up about 5 a.m. After breakfast we decided to take our chances and try the Peel. Left at 8:30 a.m., followed immediately by the "We're Here." They passed us but they ran ashore and waited till we caught up; time about 1 p.m. After taking on wood we made a fresh start. Wind is favorable and we are making fairly good time, considering we are going up a current running about 3 miles an hour. Stopped at 8 p.m., anchoring out in the stream to avoid mosquitoes. Distance about 18 miles.

Thursday, July 21, 1898

The Halifax boys and another boat caught up during the night and anchored near by. Huron passed us during the night. Up at 3 a.m. Plen [McGinnis] took the tiller and while I was making breakfast the others tracked. Had breakfast about 5 a.m. Caught up to the "We're Here" at 8 a.m. Passed the Huron at 9 a.m. with a fine breeze. Breeze kept up all day and we made fine time, covering somewhere in the neighbourhood of 30 or 35 miles. Anchored about 9 p.m.

Friday, July 22, 1898

Up at 7:30 a.m. and began tracking about 9 a.m. and kept it up till 8 p.m. Tracking fairly good and we made about 15 miles. We saw several robins.

Saturday, July 23, 1898

Up at 7 a.m. and began tracking about 8 a.m. Tracking very bad and we had to wade in 10 inches of water most of the day. Struck a bad place at 3 p.m. and after working till 8 p.m. we decided to lighten the boats to overcome the difficulty. Distance 3 miles.

Sunday, July 24, 1898

Up at 7:30 a.m. and made breakfast. "We're Here" unloaded and removed their keel and we took out about a ton. Got boats over the bad place about 12 a.m. Started at 2 p.m. and tracked till 7 p.m. Made probably about 7 miles.

Monday, July 25, 1898

Henry waked us at 5 a.m. Good wind, and immediately after breakfast we hoisted sail but could not do more than half a mile. The Imisk, Huron and two other boats are a short distance ahead. Worked from 6:30 a.m. till 6 p.m. getting over one bad piece of water. Did about 2 miles.

Thursday, July 26, 1898

Did not get up till 9 a.m. All slept in probably owing to the fact that on account of the rain last night we slept under awnings and the strong light was kept out. Started at 11:15 a.m. Dinner at 2:30 p.m. and supper at 9 p.m. Tracking today was fairly good, although we had to walk along the edge of a number of shale bluffs, and had a good deal of heavy wading. The great value of travelling with a companion boat has been fully shown the past few days. It is doubtful if either "We're Here" or ourselves could have got along without the mutual assistance rendered. Distance probably 7 miles.

Wednesday, July 27, 1898

Up at 6:30 a.m. Started at 8 a.m. Worked hard all day and I think we made about 5 miles. It is difficult to say what distances we cover daily — no two agree. Most of the day we waded, and at 6 p.m. were pretty well tired out. Passed a stake left by the Brown party and dated 19th inst., addressed to Dr. Brown, who is following with the remainder of the party. It is headed "Camp Desperation" and stated that they were having a hard time.* Mosquitoes very bad, and worry us a great deal. While hauling "We're Here" the tracking line broke and we had to go back and begin again. Millette lost his bark canoe. Distance about 5 miles.

*Editor's note: The Brown-Morse party seemed to be having more bad luck than most. At Fort Simpson, the cook of the party, J. Bouret, misjudging the depth of the water, was drowned when stepping out of the boat, his rubbers filling and weighing him down.

Thursday, July 28, 1898

Up at 6 a.m. and left camp at 8 a.m. Heavy tracking all morning. After dinner we had a reminder of the Mackenzie River by way of a very pleasant sail of perhaps an hour. We tracked till 7:40 p.m. and I was very tired. During the afternoon we missed, by five or ten minutes, a landslide on one of the shale bluffs. We could not tell the extent of the slide, but judging by the cloud of dust it raised, a very large mass must have come down. These bluffs range probably 500 to 600 feet high, and are composed of a great deal of loose material which may come down at any moment.

Passed another letter for Dr. Brown dated 22nd inst. We have gained two days on them, doing in one day what took them three days.

Passed the Enterprise between 9 and 10 a.m. Two of the crew were on board and said the rest of the party had gone ahead.

Think we covered about 9 miles today — making in all, say, 100 miles from Fort McPherson.

Friday, July 29, 1898

Up at 6:30 a.m. Began the morning's work at 8 a.m. with a very difficult piece of water — it was a rapid and we passed a rope across the stream and drew the boats up and across. Finished the job at 11:45. After dinner we began again (at 2 p.m.). After a short run we came to another rapid. We got all the boats through at 5:30, but the Halifax canoe met with an accident, and took water so rapidly that we had to discharge her load. Spent the evening with [the Springfield party]; had some guitar music and singing. Distance for the day 2 miles.

Saturday, July 30, 1898

Tracked all day and had a lot of very hard work. As we ascend the river the current increases very perceptibly, and the bad places become more numerous. Covered about 5 miles today. Decided to pass tomorrow in camp.

Sunday, July 31, 1898

Did not get up till 9 a.m. Passed the day quietly, and in the evening sang hymns. Fred Dench playing the guitar accompaniments.

Monday, August 1, 1898

Up early and began tracking at 7:45 a.m. Did a hard day's work. About 7 p.m. we came in sight of a considerable camp which turned out to be the Huron, Imisk, Idaho, Brown and Peacock parties. The three former were two days ahead of us, the latter about a week. At this point all were either busy making over their boats or had completed the job. The Brown and Peacock people are away up the river with part of their supplies and are expected back tomorrow night for the balance. We made about 8 miles.

Tuesday, August 2, 1898

Up late this morning and after breakfast began alterations in our boat, and repacking our Bovril goods which we partly damaged.* I worked on the damaged goods all day and finished the job by supper time. Cannot complete the boat before tomorrow. Do not expect to leave before Thursday. "We're Here" people are making similar alterations in their boat.

Editor's note: Bovril "concentrated" foods were apparently very popular with Klondikers. See the advertisement taken from Ogilvie's Klondike Official Guide.

Wednesday, August 3, 1898

Completed boat today and reloaded most of our goods. Opened two of our canvas boats — one to carry Millette's goods and one for our own use. We are arranging boats so as not to draw more than 9 inches. Everything will be ready by morning.

Thursday, August 4, 1898

Up at 6 a.m. Breakfast at 7 a.m. Completed the loading of canvas boats and began tracking at 10 a.m. Before completing ¼ mile we swamped one of our canvas boats (the one with Millette's goods). After getting all the boats to a convenient point, we unpacked all the wet goods to dry. Before moving again we decided to go ahead with the two large boats, leaving our two canvas boats and the Halifax boat behind in charge of Maltby. We expect to go on for two or three days and return with one of the large boats to bring up the contents of the small boats. Did a hard day's work. The current is becoming more rapid every day and the work more difficult. We worked in water most of the day, part of the time wading in water up to our waists. Made about 4 miles.

Friday, August 5, 1898

Began tracking about 8 a.m. The morning's work was very heavy. For two miles we had to track along a shale bluff and the walking was very fatiguing. We had some good tracking in the afternoon. Did probably eight miles. Camped at six p.m. and after supper we unloaded our boat and drifted back to where Maltby camped. The distance covered in two days (about 12 miles) we drifted back over in two hours and fifteen minutes.

Saturday, August 6, 1898

Up at six a.m. After breakfast we loaded the boat and started back. We had eight men on the line and one on the tiller. We covered the former two days' work in 8 hours actual work, arriving at the camp at 5:30 p.m.

Sunday, August 7, 1898

Remained in camp all day. Hendrick's party passed us at noon.

Monday, August 8, 1898

Up at 4:30 a.m. and loaded the boats before breakfast. Started up river at 7:30 a.m. with two boats. Ralph Crichton remaining behind. Half an hour after starting, the Huron, Imisk, and Idaho parties passed us, but we caught up again at noon and received some very valuable assistance from them in getting our boats past a bad piece of bluff. In the evening we all camped together. Distance for the day probably 10 miles.

Tuesday, August 9, 1898

Up at 6:30; started at 8:30. Up till noon we did some good tracking — doing about five miles, but in the afternoon we struck some very bad places with some heavy wading, and although we tracked till 7:30 p.m. we did not add more than 3 miles to our morning's work. Distance between 7 and 8 miles. Passed the Brown party cache.

Wednesday, August 10, 1898

Up at 6:30; began tracking at 8:30. Did not meet with any difficult work although we had a lot of heavy tracking. Thought we might have reached the Snake or Good Hope River last night, but did not reach it and cannot say how far we are from it. Andrew, the guide for the Imisk party, said yesterday morning that we were two "sleeps" off. We hope to reach it tomorrow. Two boats passed us today — eight men all told, with provisions for a few weeks only. They reported Dr. Brown as being three or four days back. Distance 6 miles.

Thursday, August 11, 1898

Up at 6:45 a.m.; began tracking at 8 a.m. Work was about the same as yesterday's, although we did a little better as regards distance. At 11:30 the Hendricks party passed down for another load of supplies and reported Good Hope River as about 8 miles up, and thought we could make it tonight. Camped at 6 p.m.

owing to a thunder storm. Idaho passed us at 6:15 p.m. and camped a short distance above. Distance 7 or 8 miles.

Friday, August 12, 1898

Up at 7 a.m.; began tracking at 8:45. Beginning was an ugly piece of cut bush bank about 1½ miles. Tracking was about the same as yesterday. Stopped at 12:30 for dinner and in sight of camp at Good Hope River. Reached Good Hope River at 3:30 p.m. and Huron cache two miles beyond at 4:45. Unloaded our boat and started back to old cache at 6:40. Left Dick Feltham and [Plen] McGinnis behind. Distance 5 miles.

Saturday, August 13, 1898

Reached old cache at 3 a.m. Did not go to bed till we landed. Up at 11 a.m. Loaded boat and ready to start back at 2 p.m. Doc Waterman went down to Dr. Brown's camp for mail and brought back letters for McGinnis and Maltby. Did not expect any but I feel disappointed just the same. Tracked till 8:30 p.m. and camped on a gravel bar. We lost considerable time on the way by stopping to converse with two parties on the way down. "Enterprise" party detachment that went up the River to prospect reported that they went up the West branch beyond the Wind River. Their stories to the different parties they met appear to differ. They found a few colors below Wind River, but none beyond. Beyond the Wind River, they say, the shale hills continue but they think that on the left-hand branches higher hills are found and the chances of finding gold better. This agrees with what the Indian guide Andrew says. Distance (doubled) 4 miles.*

*Editor's note: In referring to the distances as "doubled" McAdam means that the men were going back over the route to make second trips with the goods. They are also, at this point, setting up a series of "caches" to which the goods are being transported.

Sunday, August 14, 1898

Up at 8:30. Began tracking at 10 a.m. Work was pretty hard, including shale bluff tracking and heavy wading. Distance (doubled) 10.

Monday, August 15, 1898

Up at 7 a.m. Began tracking 8 a.m. Tracked till 5:30 p.m. Stopped early owing to rain. Huron party made our camp about

9 p.m. and remained all night. The work was about the same as usual. Distance (doubled) 10 miles.

Tuesday, August 16, 1898

Made a start at 8:30 a.m. with the intention of making our cache by night. Worked hard all day, at times to our waists in water and succeeded in making cache about 9 p.m. It took us 5 days to make the first trip. We did the second in 3½ days. On our arrival we found all well and a good meal awaiting us, including cariboo meat and yeast bread. The cariboo was killed by Lawson of the Idaho party about 3 miles up Good Hope River or 5 miles from camp. Distance (doubled) 12.

Wednesday, August 17, 1898

Breakfast 9 a.m. Millette and I remained behind; remainder started off with one boat (ours) with the intention of making the next cache at the head of the ramparts. We cannot tell how long they will be away as we have no idea as to the distance. Every day brings with it new reports as to the various distances. We have to travel to make Wind River and the portage to the other side of the mountains. The uncertainty creates considerable uneasiness, as even if we can make the river on the other side and should we not find gold on this side, we do not know what river it will prove to be. We hope it will be the Stewart.

Thursday, August 18, 1898

Breakfast at 9:30. Millette did not finish his washing yesterday. Promises to do so this morning and give me a chance this afternoon. While in our tent this morning a heavy gale with rain and hail, came up and blew the tent down and made a general mess. Made up a distance table today and it shows us to be approximately 160 miles from Fort McPherson or about 190 miles up the Peel River from the mouth. We have no check on these figures but think the estimate conservative, some placing the distance from the mouth as high as 210 miles. Went to bed early.

Friday, August 19, 1898

No watch in the camp and we cannot tell the time. Our stomachs however are in fairly good working order and inform us when meal hours arrive. Did the best part of my washing today.

Saturday, August 20, 1898

Did not get up very early. Not much to do. Mended my underclothing. In the afternoon Millette and I went back to see if we could get a little fresh meat. We saw the tracks of a moose and bear, but that was all. In the evenings we had a long talk. Subject: "The same law for man and woman, and equal punishment for both." It was late before we went to sleep.

Sunday, August 21, 1898

Up very late and only two meals today. Millette is a very agreeable companion and we get along well together. We do not know when our friends will be back, but we expect them any time now. They [have been] away 4½ days.

Notes on Peel River

It was with a feeling of uncertainty that we left Fort McPherson, with the intention of ascending the Peel River to the portage over the watershed. All reports up to the time of leaving Fort McPherson were to the effect that to ascend the river with supplies was an impossibility, that even the Indians made a long overland portage to save a very large part of the river. Of course, we had the information that several large boats had gone ahead, one three weeks, and this to a certain extent showed the above rumours to be partly exaggerated. From the mouth of the river to a considerable distance above McPherson very little gravel is met, the bars being mostly sand. About 50 miles above McPherson gravel is met with the sand, and gradually the bars become practically all gravel. Where does all the gravel come from? The banks are almost entirely shale and range from 300 to 600 feet high, and do not appear to contain any gravel. It must have come from the mountains, and (from reports) from some of the branches, as the main river comes from shale hills. Up to this point the gravel bars divide the river into a great many channels, many of which are very shallow. The navigable channels as a rule run along the side of the shale bluffs, but we have found good tracking on the bar side of these channels. The trees are all small — very few exceeding 10 inches. Wild fruits in places are plentiful, particularly red currants. We see very little bird life. The carrion crow and a variety of the gull being about all we see. We have seen robins and one or two small birds, but they appear to be very few in number. We have not met with animals of any kind, although we have seen the tracks of moose and bear. Later Henry [Chomiere] saw a bear, while going up to the cache at the ramparts. (I was not there.) We fired three unsuccessful shots.

Monday, August 22, 1898

Up late and nothing to do all day. Only two meals. Difficult to get firewood.

Tuesday, August 23, 1898

Rained all night and I did not sleep much. The advance guard returned this morning. They report the river as worse above than below and the ramparts as fully 50 miles off. Andrew [Smith] had a narrow escape from drowning. Three in the track line — Ralph [Crichton], Fred Dench and Andrew — were drawn off a bluff by the boat suddenly running out of an eddy with the current. Andrew could not free himself from his strap and was drawn out into the stream which at this point was very deep and rapid. He was finally gotten safely ashore. We do not propose leaving here before tomorrow morning.

Wednesday, August 24, 1898

Up early, loaded boats and started for the upper cache at 9 a.m. Passed Brown and Huron caches about 12 o'clock and had dinner at one o'clock. Camped at 6 p.m. at the same place as on the first trip. Did not find the work any harder than below, but it was quite hard enough, including a great deal of heavy wading. 9 miles.

Thursday, August 25, 1898

Up at 6 a.m.; broke camp at 7:50 a.m. Work same as usual. Camped again at same place as first trip. Made camp at 8 p.m. and was very tired.

Friday, August 26, 1898

Up at 6 a.m. Left camp at 8:15 a.m. Began the morning's work with a piece of cut bluff. It was fairly good tracking and not very long. The work continues about the same. Could not make the first trip camp, by probably a mile or so. Camped at 6 p.m. 7 miles.

Saturday, August 27, 1898

Nothing special occurred today. Tracking was about the same. We are not making as good time as on the first trip. Came in sight of the Brown camp at 4 p.m. and reached it at 6:15 and pitched our camp there. At 6:45 the Huron, et al, boats arrived and also pitched their tents. We were in all about 28 men. Distance 7 miles.

Sunday, August 28, 1898

Had a good night's rest. Did not get up till 8:30 a.m. Took a walk up the valley, about 3 miles. Took my rifle but did not see anything, although moose tracks were numerous; saw bear tracks also. Remained in camp all day.

Monday, August 29, 1898

Up at 5 a.m.; broke camp about 8:30. Hard work all day and I was glad when we ceased tracking. Water is becoming colder. We are now five days from the old cache and it will take us another day to make the upper cache. Distance 5 miles.

Tuesday, August 30, 1898

Breakfast about 7 a.m. Began tracking over a very fair gravel reach, but soon came to a very bad cross stream which we had to wade. The current was swift and in places up to our waists. Stopped for dinner a short distance from the ramparts. The water was very high and we decided to wait till tomorrow to see if it would lower. Distance 3 miles.

Wednesday, August 31, 1898

Up at 5 a.m. Breakfast about 7 a.m. After breakfast we decided to try a half load. Started with ½ load at 8:30 and after about two hours' work we reached the cache. Did not have as much trouble as anticipated. After a couple of hot pancakes and a cup of tea we started back for the supplies left behind. The return trip took 20 minutes. Reached camp with the second load at 3:15 p.m. Found Andrew quite well. During his stay at the cache he used a net and was fairly successful in catching whitefish. Will not leave for Wind River, our next point, till tomorrow. The Ramparts proved to be about the finest piece of scenery we had seen so far. The strata was twisted into all shapes. Distance 2 miles.

Thursday, September 1, 1898

This morning we loaded the boats and at 12 o'clock had dinner. We left about 1:30 p.m. Harris and Barclay, and two of the Brown party — two small boats — left one hour ahead of us.

After about two hours' hard work we began crossing the delta of the Bonnett Plume or Quartry River. It was very slow work, this river entering the Peel in a great many channels, all of which we had either to wade across or take a line over and pull the boats across. We camped in sight of our cache. Made probably 1½ miles.

Friday, September 2, 1898

Up about the usual time and began tracking at 8 o'clock. This morning we had probably one of the worst pieces of water to cross that we have yet had. We had to take both boats over by holding them up to the current instead of using the line. The water in places reached our waists. We caught up to the other two parties at noon and travelled the rest of the day with them. We camped together at night. We have rain about every day now. The trees are changing color and the leaves are falling. Made about 3½ miles.

Saturday, September 3, 1898

Up at 6:30 a.m. Began tracking at 10 a.m. Henry cleared the trees from three cut banks. Had dinner at 12:30. Rained a good part of the day. Tracking very slow. Other two parties camped at 12 o'clock, owing to the rain. We kept on till 6:30.

Sunday, September 4, 1898

Up at 10:30. Remained in camp all day. White frost in the morning. We are without a thermometer. We had one but it was broken sometime ago.

Monday, September 5, 1898.

Up at 6 a.m. Left camp at 8 a.m. The work was hard all day. The rapids followed each other in quick succession, and the wading was heavy. It rained most of the day and we did not see the sun. Taking it all together, it was probably the most miserable day we have passed. We reached the Ramparts about 6:30 p.m. and the mouth of the Wind River at 8 p.m. We expected some difficult work getting through the Ramparts, but found it quite easy. Distance 7 miles.

Tuesday, September 6, 1898

Up at 8 a.m. Unloaded boats and started back at 11 a.m. Two of the Brown party went back with us. We towed their boat behind. Made the trip down in 3½ hours. Found the remainder of the Brown party at the old cache. They left shortly after our arrival to go back for another load. We loaded our boats, ready to make an early start tomorrow. The day was very warm.

Wednesday, September 7, 1898

Began the last trip up at 8:45. Made one or two changes in our route, which lessened the labour somewhat. We worked hard all day with the result that we equalled the first day of our former trip. The day was fine but the water was cold. Camped with Moran and Harris.

Thursday, September 8, 1898

Broke camp at 8:30. Another fine day and we did a good day's work. Camped at 6 p.m. Moran and Harris camped with us again.

Friday, September 9, 1898

Broke camp at 8:45. We were again favoured with a fine day, but in spite of the warm sun we found the water very cold. We are looking forward to tomorrow when we expect to reach the cache. Camped at 5:15 p.m. with Harris and Moran, and about an hour later the Huron and Imisk parties caught up and camped with us. We are equalling our former trip although our boat is a man short.

Saturday, September 10, 1898

Up at 6:30. Other parties left first. Just before starting, Ralph Crichton saw a cariboo trotting along on the gravel bar opposite. Dick Feltham had the first three shots, his second doing the business. About fifteen or sixteen shots were fired. I fired three. We found on examining the carcass that seven shots had taken effect.* The animal, of course, was considered Dick's and he took the head and skin. The meat was divided. The incident caused us considerable delay, but it was a delay we could well afford as fresh meat is not to be had every day. We stopped for dinner at 12 a.m. and began tracking again at 2 p.m. Arrived at the Ramparts at 4 o'clock and at the cache at 5 o'clock. Found Henry and Doc [Waterman] well and glad to see us. Henry, Doc and Barclay, during our absence, went up Wind River about 6½ miles where they found a very good place for a shack. It is probable we will leave Monday for that point, for we cannot delay owing to the season advancing rapidly.

*Editor's note: The number of shots fired and the attention McAdam pays to this event indicates the excitement generated by the first cariboo and emphasizes the scarcity of game.

Sunday, September 11, 1898

In camp all day. Kendrick and Brown ("Dad & Son") parties arrived with their first loads this afternoon.

Monday, September 12, 1898

Up at 6:30 a.m. Left about 10 o'clock with our first load (all hands on the line) for the first cache up the Wind River, about 2 miles; returned at 1:30 p.m. Left at 3 p.m. with the second load (in the C.H.S. boat) and returned at 7:00. Judging by the mouth of the Wind River, it must be a very rapid river. In the two miles that we travelled up it, we found it to be one succession of rapids, showing considerable falls in each instance, probably 4 to 6 feet.

Tuesday, September 13, 1898

Miserable and cold, with rain all day. Remained in camp all day.

Wednesday, September 14, 1898

Up about 6 a.m. Began tracking at 8 a.m. Made two trips today and completed removal to the cache 2 miles up Wind River.

Thursday, September 15, 1898

Up at [?] a.m. Began tracking at [?] a.m. Arrived at Wind City at [?] p.m.* Two of the Kendrick party and one of the Idaho were there, having gone up yesterday to lay out grounds for shacks. Just before our arrival at Wind City we saw the Skin boat arrive from over the divide. They all appeared to be thoroughly satisfied with the result of their month's work. They report no portage from one river to the other through the mountains, but say that the Peel takes its rise in a broad valley and that the river running in the other direction rises close by. The guide's (Andrew's) information, given in advance, proved correct in every instance. They found a fine color on this side. We returned to the lower cache to camp.

Editor's note: The name, as McAdam makes clear at all subsequent points, is "Wind City" and was given to the spot by their party. It obviously takes its name from the river.

Friday, September 16, 1898

Made two trips to the upper cache today. We have been joined by Peacock and Barclay. We took up their supplies today in the C.H.S. boat and left the boat above and walked back. The distance is about 4 miles and the morning trip took us 2 hours 50 minutes and the afternoon trip (a much heavier load) 2 hours and 45 minutes. We expect to make two trips tomorrow and end the tracking. The afternoon trip was made in our boat and we returned in it to the lower cache to camp.

Saturday, September 17, 1898

Rained all day today and we did not move. Doc Brown, Dave Hopkins and Frank Summett arrived about noon today on their way up to Wind City with their first load. They remained here in camp.

Saturday, September 18, 1898

Rained and snowed all day and we remained in camp. So did the Brown party. Toward the evening it snowed quite hard, and things looked wintry. Another sad accident happened to the Brown party. Tim Orchard was drowned on the 7th instant. The bridle of the track line broke, and the boat shot out into the current, drawing Orchard in. He was in the water about 20 minutes and was dead when taken out. It is supposed the line hooked on to a stone and held him down. He was buried near where he drowned. A small log house was erected over the grave. This is the second drowning accident in this party. They lost their cook at [Fort] Simpson. He jumped out of the boat into what he supposed was shallow water, but it proved very deep. He was buried at Simpson.

Monday, September 19, 1898

Up at 6:30. Breakfast at 8 a.m. Four inches of snow on the ground. Loaded the boat and began tracking about 10 a.m. Arrived at upper cache about 1:30 p.m. Brought tents and camping outfit with us. We will remain here and go back tomorrow for the last load.

Tuesday, September 20, 1898

Up at 7 a.m. Left for the lower cache at 9:20 a.m. Back at 1:23 p.m. with our last load. Have named this place Wind City. Expect about 10 shacks and about 40 men to put up at this place this Winter.

Thus endeth the Track Line. Thank Heaven!*

Editor's note: 187 days have passed since leaving Montreal.

Wednesday, September 21, 1898

Up at 7:30 a.m. We began this morning cutting timber for our shack. Tomorrow we will begin putting up the logs. There will be four shacks in our group:

Peacock & Barclay

Dench & Waterman

Feltham, Crichton & Payzant

Our Party

We have a little fresh snow each day and the weather is fairly cool. We have two tents up, Millette's for sleeping and one of our small ones for cooking and dining room.

Thursday, September 22, 1898

Up at 7:15 a.m.; put up about half our shack today. The work, of course, is entirely new to me and although the work is by no means light, it is a very agreeable change, much more pleasant than tracking. It will probably take us a week or ten days to build it and we expect to occupy it about 4 months, as Andrew [the guide] says we cannot move till about the 1st of February, owing to the first part of the Winter being very stormy and the days very short.

Friday, September 23, 1898

Up at 7:20 a.m.; at 6 p.m. we finished for the day leaving only one layer of logs to put up tomorrow.

Saturday, September 24, 1898

Finished walls of the shack today and put on about half the roof.

Sunday, September 25, 1898

Up late and rested all day. Tomorrow I begin my week as cook.

Week ending October 2, 1898

Finished my week as cook. My first attempt at an apple pie was a decided failure, otherwise my cooking appeared to give satisfaction. Made my first bread from sour dough.*

*Editor's note: The Dictionary of Canadianisms *describes "sour dough" as "fermenting dough, often a piece held over from a previous baking, used as a starter in baking bread." In his notebook, McAdam states that one of the greatest hardships of the Klondike trip, for some parties, was the cooking: "Many men received their positions with the parties they travelled with owing to their representing themselves as experienced cooks." He then goes on to state that many of these men knew nothing at all about cooking and consequently "food was the greatest hardship these parties had to contend with."*

Week ending October 10, 1898*

Finished our shack on Saturday the 9th and moved everything up from the tents. Andrew, Joe, and myself began sleeping in the shack on Thursday night but continued taking our meals in the tent until the end of the week. The place promises to be very warm and comfortable. On Saturday two skin canoes arrived from up the river, three Indians in each with fresh Cariboo meat. A meeting was called to decide on standard prices to pay the Indians for what they might bring. This was thought advisable, as otherwise trouble might arise with the Indians about the prices paid by the different parties and as a result dissatisfaction which might end in their not bringing us meat. The meeting decided on the following prices. The Hudson Bay Co. one pint cup to be used as measure:

1 skin (50c)	1 cup tea
1 skin (50c)	2 cup flour
1 skin (50c)	⅓ lb. tobacco
1 skin (50c)	2 cups sugar
1 skin (50c)	1 pr. moccasins
6 skins	1 moose skin

The Indians agreed to sell us meat as under:

8 skins .... 1 carcase Cariboo

12 skins .... 1 carcase Moose

The meeting gave considerable satisfaction all round and we hope its spirit will be strictly observed. For 8 cups of tea, say 3 lbs. at 40c a lb. (including all freights), $1.20, we get a cariboo carcase, say 250 to 300 lbs., say ½ to ¾ of a cent per pound.

The hunting party arrived home today after an absence of 9 days and reported bad luck. They did not kill anything, and were compelled to return sooner than they expected owing to a lack of provisions. The weather was pleasant throughout the week. On Thursday at 8 a.m. the thermometer registered 4° above zero. I expect to try my hand at hunting shortly and so I fixed my waist belt to hold cartridges.

*Editor's note: From this point on until late January, 1899, the entries in McAdam's diary cover a week's activities; they are much longer and much more detailed.

Sunday, October 30, 1898

Have given up writing daily diary. Life is quiet and each day is pretty much a repetition of previous days. We are now fully settled in our shack and so are all the other parties.* Snow has fallen almost every day and is now fully 15 to 18 inches deep around our shacks and is said to be twice as deep in the hills. The Indians have not made a second visit yet. We would like to see them as our share of their first visit only lasted a week. The river has not frozen yet, but is gradually falling and the shores are slowly approaching each other. Hunting parties are continually going out but without success, and return without even the satisfaction of having seen fresh tracks. The snow is gradually deepening however, and if Andrew's (the Indian guide's) remarks are correct, the animals should appear very shortly in the valleys. The deep snow in the hills drives them into the low country. During the past two weeks I have made a moose skin coat and pants. They fit fairly well and I hope they will answer the work they are intended for. The bi-weekly concerts continue and show improvement as the season advances.** Our attempt to form a city government was a decided failure owing to a silly feeling on the part of a few which resulted in some ugly remarks being passed.*** Our last concert was the best so far. The singing was good and the programme was carried out without any hitch. My part in the concert was a short lecture on astronomy entitled "Primary motions of the Earth and Moon.**** Last Sunday we had a short concert of sacred music. It was held in our shack, and it is intended to repeat each

Sunday. We have secured all the wood necessary for the winter and about all the work now is to cut [up] same and bring it into the shack. Several shafts have been sunk but at a depth of about ten feet water, in each instance, came in and prevented digging to bedrock. Hope later to go deeper! Our shacks are built in a heavy spruce bush growing on what appears to be an ancient river bed. At a depth of three feet gravel is met and we think if bed rock can be reached, we might possibly settle any doubt as to whether there are any prospects on this river. We expect to begin shortly on our toboggans for carrying supplies up to the pass. Our present dull life is not all to my taste. We have not sufficient provision to admit of our sitting down and eating them and our prospects of adding to our stock of grub do not appear very bright. Most of the people here are short in supplies, and the future does not promise any means of procuring same without repeating a great deal of last Summer's hard work.

Editor's note: According to J. G. MacGregor, approximately seventy men took up winter residence at Wind City.

**McAdam later makes it quite clear that, perhaps contrary to what one might expect, the inhabitants of Wind City were not a bunch of "down-and-outs," trying to make their first success at the Klondike; among the inhabitants were four doctors, a dentist, several lawyers and some businessmen. As one of the Wind City's inhabitants put it: "Almost every profession was represented and probably at no other point in the north was social life and friendly feeling so much in evidence as at Wind City," (MacGregor, p. 160). It is not surprising, then, that the social entertainments should have included such things as lectures on the circulation of the blood or on the "Primary Motions of the Earth and Moon."

***There is, apart from this reference, ample evidence that life in Wind City was not always harmonious. George Mitchell, whose party had a shack not far from McAdam's, elaborates upon (and no doubt highly exaggerates) one such cause of discord in the highly entertaining book, The Golden Grindstone. Many of the Klondikers who had made their way up the Peel River had, states Mitchell (in his usual tone of self-importance), actually followed him on that route, feeling that he had gotten special government information about the route and the possibility of finding gold.

> *When the miners found that they would have to winter on the river a damn nasty thing turned up. . . . They now turned round and claimed that there wasn't a pass over to the Stewart, and that I'd lured them up there, and that they were going to lose a year or two years on the way and would probably all die. In fact they laid the blame for the whole God-damn thing on my head. As the days went by the men were getting uglier and uglier, and finally they held a mob-meeting and accused me publicly of having brought them all to disaster. Well, I didn't have to do it, but I knew the bad feeling*

Klondike : Complete : Outfit

------COMPRISING------

"ALASKA BRAND" EIDERDOWN SLEEPING BAGS
(WATERPROOF)

DUCK AND MACINAW CLOTHING

Such as we supplied to Canadian Government exploring parties, including Hon. Mr. Sifton and Major Walsh's, and Northwest Mounted Police for the Yukon.

Fur Lined, Leather Covered Coat.

Manufactured Wholesale by

JAMES W. WOODS

...75 Queen Street..
OTTAWA, Ont...

Lumbermen's
Supplies

Prospector's Waterproof Rawhide Boot, Laced on Side

Hood and Sleeping Bag—14 lbs.

SEND FOR CATALOGUE

Toronto Office - 85 King Street West
(DR. JAEGERS)

Montreal Office - - - 290 Guy Street

Vancouver, B.C. Office - 536 Hastings St.
J. F. CARRUTHERS, Agent

This advertisement, and the three which follow, are samples of those which would-be Klondikers like McAdam must have read. These were taken from Ogilvie's Official Klondike Guide.

Vimbos

FLUID

BEEF

(Ox-Strength in a Tea Cup)

Klondike Expeditions Need That

The ideal package for this purpose is our **16 oz. Tin with Penny=lever Top,** which can be opened and closed without injury to the tin or contents. **The most convenient and economical package;** makes **60 cups** of Fluid Beef.

Best
For Strength and Flavor

Vimbos Fluid Beef is prepared in Edinburgh, Scotland, and is guaranteed to be of prime quality.

It will pay you to write for quotations before laying in supplies.

The Vimbos Fluid Beef Co., Limited, of Edinburgh and London

CANADIAN OFFICE:

HENRY WOODLEY, Manager.   53 St. Francois Xavier St., MONTREAL.

Complete Outfits. :·:

Groceries and Provisions for Mining and Exploring Expeditions

Packed in 50 lb. bags or packages, and compressed to the smallest possible compass. (See Mr. Ogilvie's Report.) ✿✿

<u>Our Specialty</u> is Evaporated Vegetables and Fruits absolutely free from moisture, and warranted to retain their natural flavor and properties in any climate, including :

Potatoes

Onions

Leeks

Cabbage

Celery

Carrots

Etc., Etc.

Apples
Apricots
Peaches
Prunes
Etc.

Also....
Milk
Coffee
Cream
Cocoa
Etc.

✿✿Condensed and Solidified Soups, Bouillons, Beef Extracts and Fluid Beef, Etc. Every description Canned Fruit, Vegetables, Meat, Fish, Beans, Pork, Flour, Honey, Etc.

Buy at Headquarters and SAVE MONEY.

WARREN BROS. & CO.,

Wholesale Grocers and Importers, - 35 & 37 Front St. E., TORONTO, CANADA.

Portaging on the Slave River

A packer with an average load of 200 pounds

Loading boats after a portage

Some Klondikers preferred to "shoot the rapids."

Eben McAdam poses with Indian traders at Dawson.

The McAdam party on the Mackenzie River

The Ramparts, Mackenzie River

The McAdam party at Fort McPherson, July 1898

would have gone on all winter and got worse, so I just called their bluff. I got right up in the meeting and spoke.

'I don't know what you bloody fools are talking about,' I said. 'I didn't ask you to come up here and I didn't advise you to come up here. I didn't want you up here one damn bit. If you choose to butt in on my business that's your look-out — you came up of your own wills and now you can bloody well freeze and starve for all I care. But just to stop the chinmusic I'll bloody well go up to that pass myself and show you. . . . And I bloody well did go. (Graham, The Golden Grindstone, *pp. 138-139).*

Perhaps these were the very "remarks" to which McAdam alludes.

****McAdam was, according to his daughter, an avid amateur astronomer. For many years a model which he had made of the solar system was housed at McGill University.*

Sunday, November 6, 1898

Another week has passed. Eating and sleeping are now the two principal features of our living. We did some work the past week getting out birch for making toboggans. Monday and Tuesday we went up the creek back of our shacks, and cut and brought down four pieces, and on Wednesday cut three more which Joe White brought down with his dogs. On Monday I brought down two partridges with my Winchester (and Henry one). Henry made a toboggan and tested it and we think it will answer our work this Winter very well. We had two visitors from the lower shacks. A man the name of Hall [perhaps Charles Hall] from the "Lady Hamilton" party and a Frenchman named Francis of the Pat Curran party. The latter is now alone, having left the Curran party some time ago. He is here to see if we can help him to secure his full share of supplies which he is entitled to. The question came up at our last concert and it was decided not to do anything till all concerned arrive here. Francis appears to be a very straightforward man, but of course, there are two sides and anyway there are a sufficient number of men below to see that he receives justice. Unfortunately however he cannot speak English and none below can speak French, hence his reason for coming here.

Our last concert was quite a success. My part was a continuation of "Primary motions of the Earth and Moon."

Yesterday (Saturday) Andrew and myself, with shotgun and rifle, went down to our old cache below but did not see anything, or even a track. We tramped about 10 miles and as the snow is now knee deep we found the tramping pretty hard.

Tomorrow my week for cooking begins.

Sunday, November 13, 1898

Time is flying. I fully expected that time would drag, but it is the reverse. We will have been here two months next Sunday and it does not seem more than two or three weeks. The days are shortening very rapidly. The sun rises about 10 a.m. and sets at 2 p.m. My cooking week ends today. We have only had two meals a day — the first about 10 a.m. and the second between three and four. Millette does the bread baking and will be relieved from his cooking week. He makes very good bread. The Friday night concert was a pleasant affair. Dr. Brown proposed, and Ralph Crichton seconded that I be chairman. This was my first time in such a position. Dr. Brown's lecture on the "circulation of the blood" was very good and I thoroughly enjoyed it. Saturday night we held a meeting to consider several tenders for taking the mail to McPherson and the bringing back of the September mail. The meeting was a failure. Millette and Henry [Chomiere] put in a tender for $150.00 cash. There were three for $100 and one for grub only. The latter tender also included a condition, viz. were the carriers not back by the time their parties started for the divide, the citizens were to carry each a proportion of their supplies to the point their parties had reached when they arrive back. It is probable that there will be a private canvass, as several parties want to go, and a quicker and more satisfactory result can be reached this way. Saturday five of the people from the lower shacks arrived here to pay us a visit. Dad Like is billeted with us. He is quite a jolly customer!

Thursday, November 24, 1898

Nothing of any importance has occurred the past few days. Life is monotonous, and I think most of us will be glad when the time arrives to move on. The Huron people began on Tuesday to move up their supplies. The first stage is 10 miles and they made it in about 4 hours. Yesterday they took another load; today the last load for the present. They intend, however, continuing with the goods they have moved, till they reach the Swedes camp which is probably about sixty miles up the river and when the goods are there to return to the shack here and remain till February. This is what they say, but they are a canny lot of fellows and as usual are trying to get ahead of all others. The Dr. Brown party began yesterday moving their supplies and it is probable we will begin next week too. The concerts continue as usual and are quite pleasant affairs. The suggestion at the meeting regarding mail (that any who were willing to go to McPherson make a private canvass) was taken up by Doc Sloan and M. E. Putnam, and after a fair list of cash and supplies had been subscribed they decided to go and began the journey on the 16th inst. On the 20th inst., however, we were somewhat surprised to learn that they had returned. They had only reached the first shack down by the ramparts. The weather was intensely cold the morning they left, the thermometer registering 31° below zero in the early morning and 38° below zero at noon the same day (the following day there was a further drop to 51° below zero). They had a hard time of it and were compelled to leave their toboggans at the ramparts and make the first shack as soon as possible. They were accompanied by four visitors from the lower shacks who were returning and these men almost gave out and it was partly on this account that they were compelled to leave their toboggans behind in order to assist them. Several were frost bitten. This is "Thanksgiving Day", and we are to hold our concert tonight instead of Friday night. There will be nothing in the way of turkey for dinner and we will have to be satisfied with our usual meal. I wonder what our position will be this time next year? Will we be on claims? Our supplies on hand will not see us through more than six months more and I cannot but view our position in a rather serious light. Of course we have sufficient to take us to Dawson City if it comes to the worst, but we cannot afford to do that. Next summer we _must_ prospect, and will have to secure supplies of some sort to carry us over the Summer. We have not come into this country to explore a route between the MacKenzie River and the Yukon. A few nights ago (the 22nd) a meeting was held to see if arrangements could be made to send out prospecting parties, but as with our other business meetings here it will probably amount to nothing. The general desire appears to be to get over the divide as soon as possible, the impression being that there is nothing on this side. Personally I advocate trying on this side, but few agree with me. Claims on this side are 500 feet each, on the other side they are only 250 feet, not to speak of the royalty of 10%, so that claims on this side, if any, are worth twice the value of the others.

The days are growing very perceptibly shorter, and in another month or so we will have to do without old Sol for a time. The moonlight nights are very fine however. Last night the moon was encircled by several rings of various hues and presented a beautiful sight. Every clear night we have displays of Aurora and at times they are of the most brilliant order. Since last entry I have read Nansen's "Farthest North", two volumes [1897]. Enjoyed the story very much, although I had to read the two volumes in reverse order. What attracted my attention a good deal was the fact that during this month we have had almost as

65

cold weather as Nansen at any time during his absence, although he was very much farther north — about 20° farther.

Thanksgiving Day is about over and at the present moment the concert is going on but I am not there, but instead at home. I thought it better to take advantage of a quiet evening, have a bath and change my clothes. We had Joe White and Frank Sennett to our combined dinner and supper. We had more than I had expected earlier in the day. We had potatoes and onions (condensed of course) and a hash of Bovril (two combinations) and afterwards stewed rice with raisins and apricots, coffee, milk and sugar. This was a very extravagant meal, but we thought the day justified it. About four this p.m. Hopkins and Sennett returned after an absence of seventeen days. They went up the river about 25 miles to the wicki-up, and then up "Hungry Creek" about 25 or 30 miles.* Out of the seventeen days they hunted four and succeeded in killing 5 cariboo. Three of the five (out of a herd of twelve) Sennett killed.

Editor's note: Wicki-up: an Algonkian word for a "rude shelter, as lean-to" — (Dictionary of Canadianisms)

Tuesday, November 29, 1898
Linda's birthday.

Friday, December 2, 1898
The last month of the year is now fairly started. During the past, little has been done except getting our toboggans and sleds ready. Henry has done all the work and has turned out some very good work. The weather continues very cold — the thermometer persistently remaining away below zero. The claims made for the cold in this part of the world have some truth in them [seemingly to the effect that the weather is not as cold as in other countries at the same latitude], but let us hope that all who come into this country provide themselves with a sufficiency of good warm clothing as the weather is cold notwithstanding the claims made for it. During the past ten days or so quite a lot of moving has been going on and the frost bites have been numerous although nothing so far of a serious nature. Man has still a very strong strain of the monkey in him and if proof is wanted let us take any number of men, and place them together and watch the monkey side in his nature come out in his strong imitative propensities. Man is a copyist. Free-will in man is a myth. Aside from the men of will who exist and lead (and "the exception proves the rule") man may be said to exist by

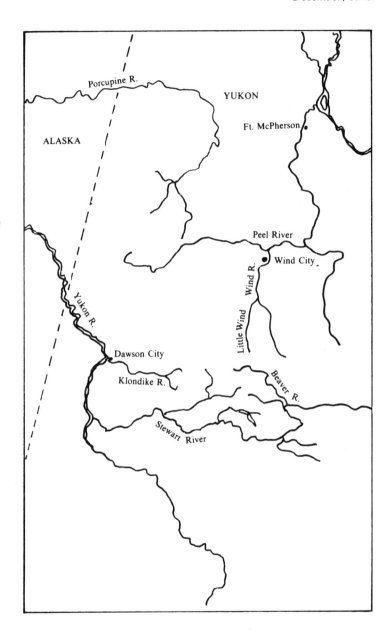

*The last stage of McAdam's journey: Fort McPherson, July 16, 1898
— Dawson City, June 15, 1899*

living on the thoughts of the few, seldom if ever reaping any benefits of their own experiences or those of others, but go blindly ahead copying blunders, and in a few instances are fortunate in meeting with success.* When we arrived here it was the intention of all — at least they said so — to remain here till about the first of February and begin then to move up the river, but the Huron party began moving a few days ago, and of course, the rest, or most of them, begin to do likewise. Time is moving along at a rapid rate and it seems impossible to realize that it is already the second of December. We fully expected that time would hang on our hands.

*Editor's note: This outburst is the first extended personal statement which McAdam makes in his diary. The long winter's monotony seems to be making him somewhat irritable and, as the following entries show, he is getting lonely.

Sunday, December 25, 1898

I have neglected my diary for a long time and think this a good day to enter it to date. There is not much to enter as life here continues about the same.

Christmas here again. What a change in a year; 4,500 miles from home and not one cheering word for nine months. Where will we be 12 months hence? In this country? Will we meet with success during the next year? What I would give to see my two little darlings today. No doubt they are enjoying themselves and perhaps thinking of me.

All our toboggans are ready and we have decided to leave our shack permanently about the 15th of January. Ten loads are cached about 8 miles up — Andrew three, Henry and Charlie two each, and the rest of us one each. We will probably move our caches about 8 miles each move, with our camp midway between, so that at no time will we be more than 4 miles from camp. This we consider advisable in order to avoid danger, in the event of storms coming up suddenly.

We had a visit from the Indians a week ago. Ten dog teams came down with meat and all here will have a good Christmas dinner. We received a good share trading shirts, sweaters, tea, &c for what we got. All teams returned loaded with supplies from the various parties here. We were foolish enough to allow several opportunities to pass but will try hard next time they come to send up 1,000 to 1,500 lbs. We took advantage, while the Indians were here, to engage two of them to carry the mail to McPherson and bring back any letters that may be there for us. All the citizens are now anxiously awaiting their return. They left the 22nd and we expect them back about the 15th of January. We raised $100 in cash and provided supplies for the round trip. I have ordered a pair of Loucheux snowshoes and a deer skin coat.*

We had three meals today: breakfast at 7 a.m., dinner at 12 a.m. and supper at 6 p.m. Andrew brought out the plum cake made by his sister over a year ago, and it went fine:

Breakfast	Cariboo steak
	Potatoes and onions
	Bread
	Coffee
Dinner	Boiled Ham
	Potatoes and onions
	Apple pie
	Plum cake
	Coffee
Supper	The remains from dinner.**

Editor's note: It is interesting to read George Mitchell's highly-embellished (and no doubt partially-fictitious) account of the Indians' visit:

One day in December, when the scurvy was about at its worst, the camp had yet another alarm of an Indian raid. Someone who had been out cutting wood rushed back in terror, with the report that a large force of Indians was advancing to the attack. The miners, who had really seen nothing of the Indians so far [not true, of course, as far as most were concerned], were still in constant dread of massacre and mutilation ("Yes, Graham, I'm afraid they are rather apt to chop up"), and the whole camp immediately fell into its usual panic. Every man who was strong enough to stand turned out under arms; everything was in an uproar, and everyone — as always on these occasions — was ready to start shooting at a moving shadow. . . .

"And I'm bound to say," Mitchell went on to explain, "that the poor devil who rushed in with the first report had some damned good reason for thinking that we were going to be massacred, what with the uncertain light of the aurora and the noise that the Indians were making as they came down the river. There were seven dog-teams strung out in a long line one after the other — that meant fourteen Indians and thirty-five to forty dogs. And if you'd ever heard seven Indian dog-teams, with the dogs howling and the Indians yelling and cracking their whips and abusing each individual dog by name — well, you wouldn't be surprised that we jumped for our rifles!

Actually, of course, there need have been no alarm at all. When the Indians reached our men they shook hands all round and a tremendous palaver began. It turned out that the whole thing was an act of kindness and courtesy on the part of the chief, Francis, who was leading the party himself. He hadn't forgotten what I had been *able to do for his wife, and now he'd come in with seven good loads of fresh cariboo meat — one was a present for me and my party and the other six were for trade with the miners. And by God we needed them for the scurvy! That fresh meat saved many men's lives, and after we got it the scurvy seemed regularly to lose its grip [McAdam later mentions the scurvy, the extent of which Mitchell also exaggerates, and at that point I will add a pertinent footnote discussing it].*

We still had the package of letters that our two postmen had failed to convey to Fort McPherson, so we asked Francis if two of his runners could take them down. He was delighted to let any of them go, but most unfortunately, before the full arrangements had been made, one of the Indians who understood a few words of English found out that we were going to have paid what they called "eight hundred skins" to our own boys, and be God-damned if they'd go for less! Otherwise they'd have gone with the best will in the world for about forty dollars! So we gave them a letter to Firth asking him to credit them with four hundred dollars, but only to pay it next year so as to ensure that they did the job properly. It was an easy enough trip, of course, for Indians: they were down to the Fort and back again almost before we knew [according to McAdam they arrived back on the 14th of January].

At last all the trading was over, and we said good-bye, and they went off; but three or four hours later the whole damn bunch came pouring back again highly incensed. Then there came quite a nasty time, but before any trouble could start we called a council, with three a side, to find out what was really wrong, and it turned out, unfortunately, that a lot of the miners had palmed off trash on the Indians in trading for the meat — bad bacon, axe-handles with faults in them, and so forth. The worst case of all was one miner who had apparently been liberal in paying for his meat with twenty-five pounds of tea; but when the Indians came to make their tea they found that it had been soaked with water and was worthless. No miner would acknowledge that he had done this trick, so we called on the Indian to pick his man. And he walked straight up to old Campbell, without hesitation! Campbell swore ignorance of the whole affair, but several of the miners knew damn well that he had had this rotten tea, so the meeting forced the old blighter to hand some of his own possessions and buy what he could from other men until he could pay the Indians up. The others were forced to pay up too, and in the end the Indians went off happy. (Graham, The Golden Grindstone, pp. 175-177).

**Here is the Christmas menu of the Cresswell party: pea soup, bacon, fried potatoes, broiled celery, pepper, salt, Worcestershire sauce, brandy; supper — sardines, marmalade, bread, cocoa.

Monday, December 26, 1898

We did not get up till late as we did not go to bed till 2 a.m. Spent part of last evening at [George] Mitchell's shack and had a good drink, the first since I left Montreal. We had music and speeches. Did not remain late as Mr. McGruder from the lower shacks was here, and promised us a spiritualist meeting in the evening in our shack. It began about 9 p.m. and lasted till 1 a.m. Besides our own party, Dr. Brown, Dr. Sloan, Judge Morse and George Dalgeish were present; McGruder called our meeting a fairly successful one. The spirits spoke quite freely. I was the only one who did not converse. Each asked a number of questions relative to the health of family and friends, and also about our prospects in the gold fields. The answers received as regards our prospects were very satisfactory. Our party is to take out $1,500,000. The spirits also told us that the river at the head of this stream is the Stewart. Let us hope that what we heard has at least some truth in it. I am, so the spirits said, to receive seven letters and some photographs when the Indians return [as it turned out McAdam received no mail at all]. "What fools we mortals are."

We have been invited to the Huron shack for another spiritualist meeting this evening.

Saturday, December 31, 1898

The last day of the year 1898 is passing rapidly away and tomorrow will see us launched into a new year with all its doubts and anxieties. There is nothing to do but hope.

Scurvy has broken out. Three cases in Wind City and eight or nine below the ramparts and with very serious prospects for a considerable increase of the trouble. The cause appears to be unknown. The doctors recognize the symptoms, but cannot account for the sickness breaking out. So far the health of our party has continued good.*

Thursday and Friday (29th and 30th) we took up loads to our 8-mile cache: three loads and four loads. I went up both days. The work is very hard, even more so than tracking. It is a steady strain from start to finish and the return trip seems more than twenty miles. Our present cache is a mistake. It is too far to go without a rest and some refreshments. After our present move, we will probably move in two 4-mile stages, with a good dinner in between. During our hauling yesterday the thermometer showed 42° below zero. My inside coat and MacKinnon's short [coat] were covered with frost, and my nose was slightly frostbitten. Today I feel very stiff.

Editor's note: MacGregor estimates that, of the nearly 1500 prospectors who left for the Klondike via the "Edmonton routes," approximately sixty-four died, and of these half died of scurvy, an obvious result of the lack of fresh food.

In Wind City itself only three miners died of scurvy, although a number were affected by it. (Mitchell claims that three-quarters of the inhabitants were affected, but this, from all accounts, seems an exaggerated figure.) McAdam's party seems not to have suffered at all and were indeed lucky, as this description of the scurvy symptoms makes clear:

> The first sign of scurvy coming on is a weakness and bending of the knees; then the upper part of the body gets emaciated and the lower limbs inflate tremendously. It's ghastly to see how they go — you poke your finger into a leg and the hole you make stays there, it doesn't fill out again like healthy flesh. Then the gums swell till the teeth drop out, and there is a most loathsome smell. . . . After the loss of teeth they generally die. (Mitchell, The Golden Grindstone, p. 167).

One of those who died of scurvy at Wind City was A. D. Stewart, a former mayor of Hamilton, Ontario, who had gained national notice in 1885 by being the citizen who, on behalf of all Canadian citizens, laid the formal charges against Louis Riel which led to his trial and hanging. Stewart's illness and death are described in his own diary and that of his companion, R. H. S. Cresswell. See MacGregor, The Klondike Rush Through Edmonton, pp. 236-243, and R. H. S. Cresswell, "Inland Trail to the Klondike," Alaska Sportsman, 29, Nos. 2-3, 5-8, 10-11, 1963.

Monday, January 2, 1899

My birthday. The New Year's day passed quietly. In the morning I paid a call to each of the shacks. The weather was mild for this country showing only zero. Friday it was 42 below and Saturday only zero, a difference of 42 degrees in less than 24 hours.

Today I began putting my clothes and sundry articles in order, preparatory to moving away from the shack. Will probably take up a couple of loads this week.

Sunday, January 8, 1899

During the week just closed we did not do any moving. The weather was not suitable. We have decided to break up house-keeping the 16th inst. (Monday) and in order to do so we must move up seven or eight loads this coming week, leaving only sufficient for six clearing loads.

Tuesday, January 17, 1899

The mail carriers arrived on Saturday, the 14th, and my disgust was great when I learned that they did not bring one letter for me. My disappointment is great, but I suppose I must bear with it. It seems remarkably strange that out of at least ten or twelve letters that I expected to receive, not one came to hand. There must be somewhere along the rivers quite a number addressed to E. McAdam. Yesterday and today I took up loads to our 8-mile cache. The weather was cold yesterday and today. Maltby had both his cheeks frozen today. The work is desperately hard on the knees and thighs, and it is a great relief to get back to our shack and sit down. It is too cold to rest on the way, as to stop for more than a ½ minute or so we are apt to get chilled. In spite of the cold, I perspire freely. Last week was my cooking week; on Saturday and Sunday I had my hands full, having five extra mouths to fill — the carriers, Neil and Peter, and an Indian named Enoch, his wife and child, who came up from McPherson with them. Neil and Peter slept in Mitchell's shack but dined with us. McGinnis wrote to the Rev. Mr. Whittaker at McPherson, asking him to send us some Indians with teams to do our hauling and as a result Enoch came up with the two carriers. He was the only Indian Mr. Whittaker could secure. They (Enoch, wife and baby) slept in our shack. We put up a curtain of canvas cutting off a corner of the shack. Annie (the wife) is a very nice little woman and spoke fairly good English. We sent up about 250 pounds with them. Neil and Peter drawing 150, and Enoch 100 with his dogs. This is all we could send as they had their own camping outfits to take along. They are to return as soon as possible with three dog teams. We bought from the Dr. Brown party (now Dave Hopkins' party — Dr. Brown, Dr. Mason, Tom Greg and W. Guch having left that party) 150 cakes of washing soap at 6¢ per cake, totalling $9.00, and we are realizing, at the rate of one skin each (or 50¢), $75.00 — only a profit of $66.00.

Mr. Mitchell has been living with us during the past week and we have engaged his company. He hurt one of his knees six weeks ago and as Merritt and Patterson are up the river, he was alone and found difficulty in attending to his various wants, and besides his knee was very painful and needed rest.* Andrew gave me a strange piece of information today and it accounts for Judge Morse, Patterson, Merritt and Coatsworth going up the river which has always seemed a strange business to me. We are both hoping the information is correct and not a hoax and that their plans can be carried out. **If the information given certain parties proves correct, and we get places as promised, then it is quite possible that our fortunes may be awaiting us within a distance of about 100 miles.

Editor's note: In his book, The Golden Grindstone, *Mitchell makes no mention of having stayed with McAdam, but makes several long* descriptive (and perhaps highly exaggerated) statements regarding his knee. From all indications, if Mitchell can be believed, he either damaged or broke his leg and kneecap about three or four times. McAdam makes mention of Mitchell's damaged knee in January; according to Mitchell he broke his kneecap in June (perhaps this was the second time). In any event, his description of how the Indians operated on his knee is worth repeating:

> Now you must understand, Graham, that surgery, among my Indians, was entirely an affair for the women. Old Colin's wife Jane, and the young girl Flora, Francis' wife, were both surgeons — old Jane had learned the Indian medicine and surgery from childhood, but strange to say, though she would examine any case and give her diagnosis, the actual cutting she would never do, being much too kindhearted. But this was very happily done by Flora, who loved cutting — the more she hurt the patient the better she liked it!
>
> ... They began to talk at me and made a great explanation which I didn't understand practically a damn word of, but Bonnet Plume, who had followed us from the place of the accident, explained to me that they were going to take the skin back and bring together the two halves of the knee-cap, which they said was broken across the centre. They began by putting on splints, before they did any cutting, with a covering of duffle and old blanketing above and below the knee that left the region of the knee itself well exposed. Then they broke some flint flakes with sharp cutting edges off a block of flint that they kept for striking lights, and Flora started her business. I asked Francis later why they had used flint flakes instead of an ordinary knife, and he said that a fresh flint flake was clean while a steel knifeblade would have been dirty.
>
> Flora made her first cut, about three inches long, inside the knee and upwards: this didn't bleed freely and what blood there was came out clotted, but it gave a feeling of relief and I urged them to press the blood out. Then she made another cut cross-ways below the knee and a third like the first, up the outer side of the leg, and after these cuts the blood came much more freely. Then she seized the U-shaped flap of skin and flesh that she had just released on the two sides and bottom and flayed it up and back, explosing the knee-cap; and just as old Jane had said, it was split right across from side to side with the two halves drawing away from one another upwards and downwards.
>
> Old Jane had evidently known what she was going to find and had set some men to make a lot of little pins out of caribou bone. Now she forced the two halves of the knee-cap together and the other little bird drove in the pins below the base of the lower half and above the top of the upper half, and then wound them firmly together, figure-of-eight, with fine strong sinews taken from the back of a caribou and pulled out to the thickness of the coarsest sewing-thread. Then they put back the flap of skin and bound it into place with thongs, without any stitching.
>
> I don't know how long all this pleasant process took: it may have been two or three hours — anyhow, it was dark all the time

except for the firelight. I tried to carry off the first part of the game with a high head — had my cutty pipe and tried to pretend there was nothing wrong. But I must have passed out more than once, as I would waken up to find little bags of moose skin with hot ashes in them in the palms of my hands, which they used to revive me when they thought I had been out too long and perhaps might not come back otherwise. (Graham, The Golden Grindstone, pp. 190-192).

**At the time to which McAdam refers (January, 1899) Mitchell and his partners are causing quite a bit of excitement by indicating that they have "secret" knowledge of the whereabouts of gold in the vicinity of Wind River. McAdam, at several points, refers to the "secret" and also to the distrust it causes.*

Sunday, January 22, 1899

Camp No. 1

Farewell Wind City! We began our journey Southward on Friday the 20th at 11:30 a.m. and reached the 9-mile point (the Brown party cache) at 3:30 p.m. It was our longest haul but our loads were not heavy. Yesterday we made four loads each (5 hauling); in all, 20 loads, and brought all our goods up from the cache 1½ miles below. To bring our camp to this point we have travelled (I have at least) 60 miles loaded and 51 miles light; in all 111 miles. This is truly horse work but we must get there. Our weather keeps cold but so far I have escaped frost bites. The morning we left, Mitchell said he would probably write us and send the letter up with the Indians. Mitchell did not speak to me about the information; Andrew informed me of [it], although he is one of the parties in the secret. Is his letter to be the one for us to act?*

Editor's note: McAdam is clearly worried at this point and perhaps doubtful that any gold will be found. From here on in the diary there are many such doubts expressed and indeed they were justified, for none of those who were in Wind City (or indeed any of those who went by the Edmonton routes) found any gold. The secret is beginning to cause some dissension and McAdam later remarks on this, to the effect that he should have chosen better companions. Some time later the partnership was dissolved.

Thursday, January 26, 1899

Camp No. 1

Yesterday we took our last loads up to our 4½ mile cache and intended leaving today with our camp outfit for a point 8 miles up, but finding our bottle of mercury frozen, we decided that it was too cold to shift camp. The Hamilton party came up with loads and informed us that the thermometer registered, when they left, 47° below zero. Mitchell has had another accident to his knee and it is now much worse. He fell just in front of the shack. Dr. Mason was up with him two nights, and his knee is now in splints.*

*Editor's note: George Mitchell certainly is a much-less heroic person here than he appears to be in his book, The Golden Grindstone. *In the book, in fact, his injuries and incapacities are hardly mentioned. Mitchell never did make it to the Klondike, in spite of his bragging. On June 20, 1899, R. H. S. Cresswell met Mitchell on his way home, along the same route: "Met Indians on their way to the fort with their winter furs, and Ed Harris and Mr. Mitchell of Toronto and four Chicago men on their way home. Half of Harris's foot is missing (Mitchell had removed part of Harris' foot after serious frostbite and gangrene) and Mitchell's leg is in splints. Gave Harris a parcel (bed and gun) to take home for me, and traded old clothes to the Indians for two hundred pounds of dried meat."* Alaska Sportsman *[November, 1963], p. 34).*

Friday, January 27, 1899

Camp No. 2

We left camp No. 1 this morning at 10:45 a.m. and arrived here at 2:30 p.m. Distance about 8 miles. I had on about 150 pounds and the load was quite heavy enough. We had to make a new camp and as the snow was very deep, we had quite a job. The weather was not very good. The present camp is 16½ miles from Wind City.

Monday, January, 30, 1899

Yesterday was Sunday and about the only work we did was to get firewood. This a.m. we went down to the lower cache (3 miles) and after dinner continued with the same loads to a cache 4 miles up. In all we travelled about 14 miles. I am gradually getting hardened, but do not think it possible for my muscles ever to grow accustomed to such horse work. Distances cause a great many arguments in camp — no two agreeing on the distance between any two points. My table of distances travelled is not based on the time [it takes to] draw loads, but on air trips made without loads, when we are less liable to exaggerate. Another fruitful source of discussion in camp is "what we will eat when we get home" [i.e. either Dawson City or back home to Montreal]. It is really amusing to hear the many terms of disgust at our present style of eating, and all about the different favourite dishes of those present. To judge by some remarks, it is more than probable that a great many people at home will have to do without their favourite dishes, if some of the people here are to have their appetites satisfied.

Tuesday, January 31, 1899

[Got] up a little late this morning, but made our trip to the lower cache. On my return, I was overjoyed to find eight dog teams in camp, including two of our own men, Enoch and Peter. Neil did not come down, but we expect him in two or three days. Coatsworth accompanied them. After an hour's rest and some tea, Coatsworth continued on to [Wind] City with six teams. Our two men remained and after dinner went down with us to the lower cache and cleared it out. Tomorrow they will go up to the Wicki-up with three boats and fittings for the same, and cache them for the present, then return and load for the Bear River [which is] up the river at the 100-mile point. It would appear that Mr. Campbell told McGinnis about the affair Andrew spoke of to me, and tomorrow or the next day, when Mr. Campbell and Mr. Mitchell will pass on their way up, Coatsworth said that they would stop and talk the matter over. We are all anxious to hear what is to be told and are hoping that the news is good.

Thursday, February 2, 1899

Camp No. 3 "Wicki-up"

Left camp no. 2 at 9:50 a.m. and reached this camp at 1:15 p.m. Distance 8 miles. The hauling was very hard although my load did not exceed 150 pounds and the day was fine. The snow is granulated and offers great resistance to the free running of the toboggans. We expect to find the work easier when the sun is higher, but we have a month of this work still to do before we can expect any assistance from old Sol.

Mr. Campbell and' Mr. Coatsworth made the through trip from Wind City to here today, arriving at about 5:45. They will stop in our tent tonight.

Friday, February 3, 1899

Last evening I had a talk with Coatsworth re the matter referred to in late notes, and he informed me that the Indians have given proof of gold in this country. He has seen black sand samples showing what he thinks would prove good pay. He also has very fine samples of rich quartz. The Chief (Francis) has promised to show Mr. Campbell the ground and they (Mr.

Coatsworth, Judge and the Mitchell party) are anxious to have us join them and be benefited, should the information prove of any value. Coatsworth advised us to send forward two of our party so as to arrive in say about two weeks, but we have not yet decided what to do. We can't very well spare any at present.*

This morning we got the Indians off and they carried away 650 pounds. This, with about 450 pounds (three boats and oars and fixing) which we will cache here for the present, will relieve us of about 1100 pounds. We will now be able to move camp about every 5 days, 8 miles each move. We hope to reach the Swedes (about 52 miles from Wind City) by the 1st of March.

Made two trips to the cache today, in all about 16 miles. The trip in the afternoon was very bad. A regular storm prevailed and the trail filled in. I had on about 160 pounds and it was all I could do to haul it.

This morning we saw a wolf. He was prowling in camp, and when we approached he made for a clump of willows out on a [sand] bar. When returning from our cache this afternoon we were favored with a view of four cariboo about 800 or 900 yards distant. The wind was favorable to them and they made off.

Editor's note: The suggestion made by Coatsworth was that some of McAdam's party should travel with him (and others) up the Bear River where, according to Indian reports, there was substantial evidence of gold. McAdam seems reluctant to believe the reports and, indeed, they turned out to be quite false. Those, like Mitchell, who did spend time searching in that area wasted a great deal of time.

Sunday, February 5, 1899

Yesterday we brought up our last loads to this cache (No. 6). Joe [Millette] and I made only one load; the other three made two loads. McGinnis has been our cook since we left Wind City, but struck today and wants some other one to take his job. I do not think there will be any difficulty in providing a substitute, as it is certainly the easiest job on the road. I forgot to mention in my last entry that Coatsworth said that all the parties ahead of us suspect what is going on ahead, and are rushing forward, and Joe told us yesterday that Larin of the Curran party said that Mr. Campbell had told Curran what he told us, so that the secret is very far from being a secret.*

Today is Sunday and we are resting.

Our next stage is about 25 to 30 miles long and will require 4 camps — the stage is from here to the Swedes' camp. While I am still hopeful at times, I cannot but feel that the future is a very dark page. I do not permit myself to base any hopes on the reports of rich gold 75 miles up the Wind River from here. If it proves to be true we will certainly be very fortunate, but on such a trip as the present, disappointments should be avoided as much as possible.

Editor's note: That phrase, "the secret is very far from being a secret," is an archetypal one for the Klondike era. No "secret" ever remained a secret for long; what was a "secret" or very often a "rumour" one day could, a day later, result in a stampede of miners to the "secret" spot.

Monday, February 6, 1899

9 a.m. We cannot leave with our first loads to the next cache yet. The mercury is frozen. An hour ago it was not frozen, so that a cold wave has come up, or increased inside an hour. We noticed that it was very cold when we got up, but did not think it was so cold.

We have had a good many arguments of late on the subject of the Indians of this country. I am not in love with them by any means, but if we are to judge them by civilized standards and take the late citizens of Wind City as fair samples of civilized life, then to my mind they are superior to us.

11 a.m. The mercury has thawed out and we are about to start.

We made two short trips today, 2¼ miles up.

We found a stake two miles up, left by Hanson stating that there is a good camp up 4½ miles and that Little Wind River was only 12½ miles farther. The latter piece of news was welcome as were under the impression that Little Wind River was about 25 miles from the Wicki-up, instead of only 19 miles.

We have now had a pretty fair experience in living out with the thermometer lower than 42° below zero (mercury freezes at 42° below). It is suprising how comfortable a tent is in the very coldest weather, providing a good fire is kept up. It is only necessary to let the fire go out for a few minutes, however, to have the temperature the same as outside. The cold during the night is very uncomfortable at times. I have arranged my bed as follows: below rubber sheet; double blanket folded into six thicknesses and sleeping bag on top (outside canvas bag next to a blanket bag and then wolf bag inside). When I cover my head, breathing is very difficult and I am compelled at times to uncover my head to get air. I have fallen asleep on several occasions with my head out, with the result that I have been awakened by the cold, with my nose almost frozen. One great trouble is to keep our blankets dry. Our breath condenses on the blankets and they are always wet around our heads.

Wednesday, February 8, 1899

Moved camp today 6½ miles. Left at 9:50 a.m. and arrived here at 1:50 p.m. We were on the way four hours. When we left the mercury was frozen and we think the thermometer was below 42° all day, but we cannot tell till Doc Mason comes up, when we will get the registrations for the past two weeks. It was certainly one of the coldest days we have been out. The trail for most of the way was filled in and the hauling was simply desperate. My load was about 180 pounds and it was all I could do to haul it. Henry, Joe, and the Dad Brown party broke the trail. We made camp at the point indicated by Hansen. It was very cold work pitching the tent and we were all glad when we had a good fire going. Dad Brown says this is not horse work, but jackass work. Some time ago we decided not to travel in weather like the present, but all our good resolutions fall before the desire to push on.

Thursday, February 9, 1899

Could not do much work today as the weather was too cold. The mercury was frozen all day. Henry, Andrew and myself went down to our cache and brought up loads — we were short of provisions in camp and were compelled to go down. McGinnis and Joe got the wood. Maltby is cooking this week. When I got up this morning, the head of my blanket was heavily coated with frost.

Friday, February 10, 1899

Not moving today — mercury is frozen. This is a very long cold spell and is causing us some delays.

Saturday, February 11, 1899

Not so cold today, and we made two trips each to the lower cache. I brought up 195 pounds and 260 pounds. The latter is my heaviest load to date and I do not intend to repeat it. Ralph [Crichton] and Brien [?] came down today from the Swedes camp to get their mail.

Sunday, February 12, 1899

Contrary to our rule we worked today [Sunday], but only made one load each. Owing to the intensely cold weather Thursday and Friday, we were compelled to leave all work not absolutely necessary and finished bringing everything to this point. Ralph told us last night that there are four parties at the Swedes — Craigee & Smith, Gecks, Putnam and their own party. The distance to the Swedes is 18½ miles. Weather permitting we will probably reach this point about the 1st of March.

Monday, February 13, 1899

This is my week to cook. At first we thought McGinnis would do all the cooking while the rest were hauling, but for some reason he threw up the job about a week ago. It is a little over three weeks since we left Wind City and I feel like having a little rest. I am quite stiff. We are all quite well which is somewhat surprising to me considering the work.

The Indians should be down in a few days now, and if we can succeed in getting three loads more off our hands it will be a great help.

Tuesday, February 14, 1899

The Indian Enoch returned last night for another load. He had five borrowed dogs and left this morning with 400 pounds (price paid: 30 skins; no cash — all trade). I was much disappointed to learn from him that neither he nor Peter took our last loads to the point agreed on, viz Francis' camp, Bear River, but to Joseph's camp 20 miles this side. He insisted that McGinnis told him the morning they left to cache at Joseph's camp. He brought us down five cariboo quarters and a liver. He is to come back again as soon as possible.

Wednesday, February 15, 1899

We broke camp this morning at 9:30 and reached Camp No. 5 at 3 p.m. Distance 7½ miles. My load was between 180 and 190 pounds, which was far too heavy for the heavy trail. I was pretty tired when we arrived at the place to camp. Henry, Joe and McGinnis went ahead and when we appeared on the scene the tent was up. A mile and a half from the last camp we ran along the edge of a bluff about 25 or 30 feet high, and below the river ran quite open and summer like. The trees in the vicinity were heavily covered with snow, and the whole presented one of the strangest, and at the same time beautiful, scenes we have seen this winter. We are now drawing close to the mountains and our next cache will be at Little Wind River, and our next camp two miles beyond. I find cooking this week a great improvement on hauling a toboggan and cannot but wonder at McGinnis for giving up the job.

Sunday, February 19, 1899

Today I finish my cooking week and tomorrow take to hauling again. Everything is now at the upper cache and tomorrow we move camp to a point two miles beyond Little Wind River. The loads taken up by the Indians are gradually reducing our supplies here. At present we have three loads each of 170 pounds and we are enabled to move camp every four days. Expect Enoch down in a day or so for another load. Our progress is fairly satisfactory.

Monday, February 20, 1899

We broke camp today at 9:20 a.m. and reached Camp No. 6 at 2:30 p.m. For about three miles we had to break the trail; the remainder was fairly good. We had to contend with a bitterly cold wind the whole way, and most of us suffered from frost bites. Maltby had his chin frozen, McGinnis his nose, and myself my cheeks. We are now right in the hills, and the wind blows almost continuously. My moose skin suit protects my body, but I suffer a good deal in my face and hands. Today was probably the worst day we have had yet, and we made a mistake in passing the 6-mile camp mentioned by Ralph Crichton. This necessitated the making of a new camp ground 1½ miles beyond, and before our fire was going I was pretty well chilled.

Enoch arrived while we were making camp. He is a good fellow, and always lends a willing hand without being requested. He will take up a load tomorrow. We have now to pay him two skins for large quarters — the men above are doing so.* The last meat he brought proved a very acceptable addition to our meals. He brought us down this trip about 40 pounds of meat (cariboo) for which we paid him six skins, $3.00.

8 p.m. The mercury is frozen.

Distance today 7½ miles.

*Editor's note: Lest the reader has forgotten the prospectors' method of payment (outlined earlier), one skin is equivalent to 50c. The Indian would state his price in skins, and would be paid either in the equivalent cash or in goods.

Tuesday, February 21, 1899

We did not do any hauling today; the wind was worse than yesterday and we did not care to face it. Enoch did not start either, for the same reason. Henry went down to the cache in the morning and brought up 450 pounds with the dogs, and Enoch brought up 430 pounds after dinner. Dad Brown, Enoch and myself went out cariboo hunting this morning. We climbed a very high hill and found numerous fresh tracks. Dad and I could not keep up with the Indian and returned. The Indian continued on and returned half an hour later. He saw a herd of about 20 a long distance off. He brought back a martin skin. We had a magnificent view of the mountains from the hill. Eastern snow shoes are of no use whatever in this country. We had a desperate experience with them today. It was simply impossible to climb the hill at anything like a fair rate of speed and it was largely on this account that we could not follow the Indian who wore the Loucheux shoes.*

*Editor's note: According to one expert, the snowshoes worn by the Loucheux (Athapaskan) Indians were of two types: "The first, called hunting snowshoes, were long and rounded in front, and were used for walking over fresh snow. The second type, travel snowshoes, were shorter with a pointed and sharply upturned front end. These smaller snowshoes allowed the wearer to sink more deeply into the snow and were used for walking on a previously broken trail, or, in later times, to break a trail for a dog team." (James W. Vanstone, Athapaskan Adaptations, p. 26). It seems certain that what McAdam referred to as the "Loucheux" snowshoe was that with the upturned front end; the consistently flat "Eastern" snowshoe would have made travel uphill very difficult.

Wednesday, February 22, 1899

We made two loads today to the cache and finished it. The two trips made 20 miles and represents our greatest mileage for one day's work, up to this point. Distance is too great and the strain too much — 16 miles should be the limit. We are now three miles from the Swedes' camp, and will make two loads to that point tomorrow and move camp next day.

Enoch left this morning for Joseph's camp with 350 pounds.

Thursday, February 23, 1899

We finished drawing up the upper cache today; we made two loads. We expect Enoch down again tomorrow and we will leave his load here and let him come down for it. We will probably not reduce our loads any more, but make arrangements for Enoch to take whatever is now at Joseph's camp up to Francis' camp at Bear River. Tomorrow we will move our camp up to Swede's shacks, 3½ miles. Our upper cache is ½ mile this side of Swede's and we expect to move camp in the morning, and in the afternoon move up the cache. In the distance table I have called today's run 3½ miles, including the ½ mile yet to move, in preference to splitting same into two runs.

Of late we have had an abundance of cariboo meat, and it is without doubt the finest meat I have ever tasted. For the present we roast it only and find it much more tender and the flavour finer. Joe started first this afternoon, and a mile and a half up got within 200 yards of four cariboo, but of course he didn't have a rifle.

Friday, February 24, 1899

Camp No. 7 Swede's Shacks

We left camp no. 6 at 9:30 a.m. and reached here at noon. This is the shortest camp-move we have made. We thought it best to make this move as this place is a fresh starting-point and we will drop into camping places made by those ahead. Enoch arrived at noon today and will leave again tomorrow.

Dad Brown killed three cariboo this afternoon about one mile above our last camp. They were part of a herd of about thirty. We went down and brought them up to this camp, and Dad gave us a whole carcase.

Everything [all the goods] is up to this point now.

This afternoon we decided that four should go ahead as fast as possible to Bear River and find out what is going on [i.e. regarding the rumors of gold]. If reports are true, they will stake claims for all and two will return immediately, the other two remaining to protect our interests. Enoch told us that one of the Indians told him that Coatsworth was very pleased. He also told us that Doc Brown (and we presume the party he is associated with — White, Senate, George and Ferguson) have started for the Pass. What does it mean? Have the Indians kept the information from them owing to Doc Brown's treatment?*

Editor's note: Doc Brown, formerly of the Brown-Morse party but now with a smaller party, has obviously treated the Indians badly. There is, however, nothing in McAdam's diary or in any other source to indicate the nature of that treatment. Perhaps Doc Brown was simply smarter than some other prospectors and knew that to prospect at Bear River would be a waste of time.

Saturday, February 25, 1899

McGinnis, Maltby, Henry and Millette left this morning with Enoch for Bear River. Andrew and I remain, and Fred Dench will camp with us for the present. Cannot say how long they will be away, but we do not expect to hear from them for a week at least. Andrew and myself will have a good rest, as we do not intend to do any hauling while alone.

Sunday, February 26, 1899

Sunday, and a beautiful day! When we got up the mercury was frozen. This is one of the most remarkable winters I have ever passed. Not owing to the novelty of the position, but the wonderful steadiness of the weather, and its unwavering determination to keep cold — in the neighbourhood of the forties below zero.

I am doing the cooking while the others are absent.

Today Andrew is attending to the thawing out of one of the cariboo carcases in order to skin and quarter it. Lyman Brown and he are in one of the Swede's shacks performing the operation.

We are camping under canvas in preference to using either of the two shacks [it is clear from this remark that the Swedes have moved on].

We expect the Indians tomorrow about noon. They are going down to Wind City, and will proably stop here on their way down. Enoch said he expected them at Joseph's camp Saturday night and that they would remain there over Sunday.

I wonder what will be the outcome of the trip to Bear River? Will the news be good and is our fortune awaiting within 50 miles? I am hoping it is true, but am fully prepared for disappointment.

How I long to hear from home. We are now nearly a year out, and I have not received a solitary letter. Would give almost anything for a few words from my little daughter. Where can all the letters be that were sent me last Summer?

The mileage to date since leaving Wind City is: with loads 207; without loads 157½; total mileage 364½; actual distance 49½ miles. The work represented in the above figures can only be appreciated by those who have gone through a similar experience. In addition to the severe strain of hauling, we have to contend with extremely cold weather. Fortunately we do not suffer any discomfort about the body as the exertion, in spite of the cold, is sufficient to keep us warm; in fact, to cause copious perspiration. Our faces and at times our hands suffer, but up to the present no serious frost bites have occurred in our party.

The work this winter is showing up the capacity of each man to do his share of work. On the track line last summer it was possible for men to make a great show of work but in reality to be doing very little. Instead of all drawing on one line, each draws his own toboggan and the work being done is easily estimated. It is probable that a good many of the opinions formed last summer as to the quantity of work being done by some members of the party have suffered considerable change. Revenge is sweet and I am having mine now.*

Editor's note: A curious phrase — "I am having mine now" — and one which we wish McAdam had been more explicit about. In his previous entry he stated (and it seemed to be almost petulant), "Andrew and myself will have a good rest, and we do not intend to do any hauling while alone." It seems likely that one (or more) of those members of the party who had gone prospecting on the Bear River was not pulling his weight. Was it Maltby? It is difficult to say, but in subsequent entries McAdam does not mention him very often. When the party finally broke up, after reaching Dawson City, only Andrew Smith stayed with McAdam.

Thursday, March 2, 1899

We are still waiting and killing time, eating, sleeping, smoking and getting wood. We have not heard from up river yet. The Indians did not come down as expected.

The Curran syndicate arrived here yesterday.

The temperature still continues very low and the mercury freezes every night, which means at least 42° below, but how much more we cannot tell.

I went out Monday and Tuesday afternoons with my rifle, but did not see anything. The first day I climbed a hill to get a good view. Heard several wolves howling and called them, but they would not show themselves.

Sunday, March 5, 1899

On Friday, the 3rd, Henry and Joe returned from Bear River and brought with them eight dog teams to take us through, bag and baggage, to Bear River. The same afternoon five of the teams started back and the next morning (Saturday) we broke camp and began our journey at 10:30 a.m., and reached Joseph's camp, 12½ miles, at 2:30 p.m. We could have gone farther, but the next camp is 7½ miles, and this distance was too great to cover, and leave us time to pitch camp; the Indians said they wanted to remain here over Sunday. So we are here till tomorrow (Monday, 6th) and will not reach Bear River till Tuesday.

The report brought down was not by any means cheering, and the probability is that we will have to go over the pass to find gold. All the parties are passing Bear River and making for the pass which is 46 miles farther on. Campbell, Coatsworth, Morse, Merritt and Patterson are still at Bear River, and their object in remaining there is somewhat obscure. They promised to tell McGinnis full particulars at the first opportunity, and as McGinnis and Maltby are still up there they will probably have some information for us when we get there. The Indians certainly know where there is gold, but they now, according to the report brought down, refuse to make known the place until they see Mr. Whittaker, the missionary at Fort McPherson.

At this point (Joseph's camp) there are two teepees occupied by three families — six adults and about a dozen youngsters from six years of age down. Joseph holds services Sunday morning and evening in his teepee — Episcopal. Henry and Andrew attended in the morning, and Andrew and myself in the evening. They have the Bible printed in their own language (Loucheux), also the prayer book and hymnal. Joseph laid down the law in grand style. By special request, the two of us sang, repeating each verse after them. Their teepees are different from any I have seen so far — at the base they are about 24 feet, and stand about 9 feet high at the centre. In the centre is the fire pile, and there is an opening on top for the smoke to get out and a small draft opening on the floor line which causes the fire to burn very freely, and in consequence the smoke is almost unnoticeable. The covering of the frame work is skin. Three or four families often live in one of these institutions.

Editor's note: This is the first time McAdam has been explicit about the habits of the Indians in the area. The Loucheux (French for 'squinters') tribe of Indians belonged to the Kutchin group of tribes of the Athapaskan nation. The term 'Loucheux' may here be used to describe all the Kutchin Indians, as the Hudson's Bay men did. The Kutchin inhabited the region of the Yukon and its tributaries — the Peel River basin and the lower Mackenzie valley. John Franklin met them on his famous voyage to the Polar Sea and describes them in his Journey to the Shores of the Polar Sea in the Years 1819, 20, 21 and 22 *(London, 1823), as does Sir John Richardson in his* Arctic Searching Expedition *(London, 1851). In fact, the picture which Richardson provides of a Kutchin winter scene contains a teepee exactly like the one McAdam describes here. At the bottom of the page for this entry McAdam drew a small sketch of the teepee and the resemblance to that in Richardson's picture is quite apparent.*

Monday, March 6, 1899

Broke camp at 9 a.m. and reached next camp at 2 p.m. Distance 15 miles. From Joseph's camp we have four dog teams,

A Kutchin winter scene, 1840s (from J. Richardson, Arctic Searching Expedition, *London, Longman, 1851, Frontispiece).*

having secured the Indian Neal who owed us a load. There is nothing behind now. After one hour's run we fairly entered the mountains, and are now surrounded by them. At times the scenery is magnificent, and their name [Rocky Mountains] is fully justified, at this point at least where they are nothing but huge masses of rock.

Tuesday, March 7, 1899: Bear River

Broke camp at 8:30 a.m. and reached here at 12:30 p.m. Distance 12½ miles. Found Maltby and McGinnis on the ground, and were settled after about an hour's work, using Hopkins' ground. There are here, at present, Campbell, Coatsworth, Morse, Merritt & Patterson, Craigie & Smith (Jack & Jill), Ralph Crichton, Fred Payzant, Dick Feltham, Peacock & Barclay, Lanonette, Vincent, and Fritz. Several parties are ahead — the White-Sennett party of five are at the pass.

We are all glad to be here, as we now consider ourselves over the worst part and can easily do the rest of the distance, viz. about 50 miles to a point 10 miles the other side of the pass.

In the afternoon Henry and myself went up to the Chief's (Francis) camp. There are four teepees, and in all proably 35 souls.

Distances from Wind City to date: loaded, 247; without loads, 157½; total, 404½. Actual distance 89½.

Wednesday, March 8, 1899

Up late this morning, as we had not much to do today. Indians came down about 10 a.m. for settlement of their bills. We were about three hours settling with them and were glad when through. While they show considerable shrewdness, in many respects they are children. We did not part with much money, not having any too much, but traded off sundry articles of clothing, &c, that we did not require. What they fancy they will pay high prices for, but cannot be induced to what they do not want.

Game is reported as very plentiful above here.

Thursday, March 9, 1899

Our first anniversary

One year ago today we left home in search of gold, and although we have travelled in the neighbourhood of 4500 miles, we are still travelling and must do so for some time longer. In about a month or five weeks we will be over the divide and in what is claimed to be one of the richest regions of the world. We are all more or less tired of travelling and are anxious to get into the gold country and begin prospecting.

We have three more Indians to settle with today and then we are, I hope, completely through with them. They are a difficult people to get along with. Most of them have a smattering of English, and sometimes we suspect they know more of our language than they choose to let us know. Prices for transportation and meat are continually varying, and always in their favour — short hauls often costing more than long hauls. Of course, we can usually manage to equalize matters by increasing the prices for the articles we have to trade, and in several instances have done so with a vengeance.*

Editor's note: This last statement is somewhat untypical of McAdam who, in all his previous descriptions of the Indians, has been very favourable and he seems to have been otherwise quite fair in his dealings with them.

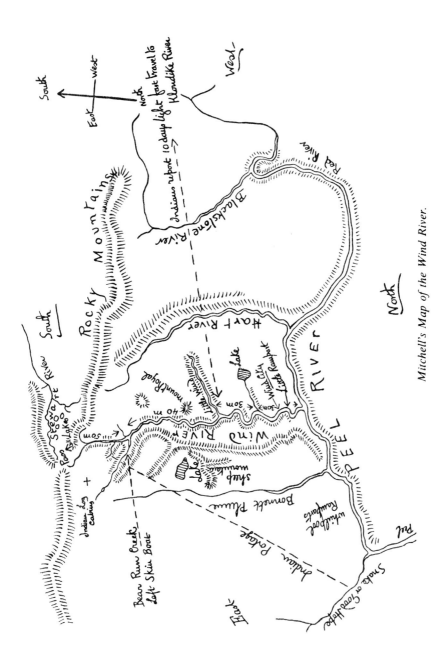

Mitchell's Map of the Wind River.

90

Friday, March 10, 1899

We began again today to haul loads, and once more have all our supplies to handle. Our present camp is up Bear River about a mile and instead of making a long circuit around we hauled all our supplies across a large bar and cached on the back of Wind River. Distance 1¾ miles. Tomorrow we break camp, but cannot say yet how far from here our next camp will be; everything depends on the wood supply. Tonight Henry is shoeing our toboggans with grizzly irons — by doing so we will be able to draw 300 lbs. per load and save many trips.* Our next stage is from here to Three Rivers, a distance of about 30 miles and there is little if any snow on the ice.

Today we had a fair sample of the wind in this region and I cannot say we enjoyed it. For some time it has been blowing from the North, and as the temperature has been very low of late it makes working outside very uncomfortable.

*Editor's note: A grizzly (besides being a bear) is a device used in placer mining and is defined by the Dictionary of Canadianisms *as "a set of parallel steel bars or rails." The "grizzly irons" referred to by McAdam were obviously part of their mining equipment.*

Saturday, March 11, 1899

Broke camp at 10:30 a.m. and reached camp No. 11 at 4:30 p.m. After crossing a large bar (1½ miles long) with our camp outfit, we added to our loads from the cache making them up to about 300 pounds (mine was 375). The camp move was a short one, about 7 miles and it took us a long time to make it owing to the loss of time in searching for places to pass the overflows.

The ice on this river must be of great thickness. Besides the freezing down towards the bottom, the water is continually overflowing to the extent of two or three inches at a time and freezing. At the present time this part of the river is almost entirely glare ice and we can easily draw 300 to 400 pounds.

Sunday, March 12, 1899

In camp today and not doing any hauling. We are running short of fresh meat, so Henry and I went out this morning on a little hunting expedition. We came across the tracks of a large herd and saw traces of where several had been killed. We returned without seeing anything.

March 13, 1899

Started out this morning with the intention of going down to the cache for loads, but we had to return owing to the high wind

which we would have to face on our way back. Maltby, Henry
and Andrew will cache 600 pounds here, up at where the Gecks
are camped about 1½ miles. Made another start this afternoon,
but were compelled to return as we could not possibly do any
hauling against the high wind.

Tuesday, March 14, 1899

Today we are again storm-bound and feel much provoked at
the delay. There is probably lots of time to get over the divide,
still what work is to be done we want to do now and rest after.
Henry and Andrew went out this morning to look up some
cariboo but returned unsuccessful.

Idleness does not tend to improve man's spirits, but rather to
give him time to brood over past and future troubles, with very
often the result that life for the time being is simply unbearable.
I often feel that my disposition is changing very rapidly and
much more so since I left home. I fight against this feeling, but
fear I do not win very often. As a party we are not suited to each
other and time is not improving matters. As a whole, I do not
regret the trip, as it is too early to despond, but had I to begin
again, I should certainly give more attention to the choice of
partners.

Thursday, March 16, 1899

We started out yesterday morning for the lower cache, leaving
at 7:15 a.m., but did not go down more than 2 miles. We had to
return owing to high winds. Henry and Charlie went down,
however, and brought up loads. Henry had on creepers and
could walk on the ice. He had to haul his own load and Charlie's
most of the way. Andrew, Joe and myself made a second start
about 10:15 a.m. Joe returned, and Andrew and I continued. We
could not face the wind to return, so we went over to Peacock's
and waited till 5 p.m., hoping that the wind would drop. We
went to the cache at 5 p.m. but the wind was so strong that we
returned to Peacock's and remained there all night. Fred Dench
arrived at 9:15 p.m. Left for the lower camp at 10 a.m. and on
reaching it found Henry, Charlie and Joe there. We returned
together bringing up everything. Henry wore his creepers again
and had to help all round. It is almost impossible to stand on the
ice, the wind the past few days has polished it and made it
smoother than glass. The temperature the past few days has risen
considerably and it is now comparatively warm. Fred Dench
brought up some very bad reports from Wind City. They came
directly through miners, so will probably be correct, although we

hope not. Charles Mills of the Hamilton party had to return to Wind City with Harris (same party) with a very badly frozen foot. Think it will have to be amputated.* Doc Mason is seriously ill at Wind City. One of the Bourman brothers, Wind City, is not expected to live and the other brother is very sick. Billy Guch is down with scurvy.

The only piece of good news is that Mitchell is well again.

*Editor's note: This is how George Mitchell describes Harris' calamity:

Harris and I had gone up the river to cut fire-wood, and were coming back dragging our loaded toboggans. Harris was ahead, but not far enough ahead for safety, and suddenly the ice gave way and put us in the water five feet below. The river had dropped, you see, and left the ice and snow without any support. Luckily it was a piece of dead water, so we weren't drawn under the ice, but we were pretty wet about the feet and legs. I made a beeline for the bank, where I saw some dry brush and tree roots, and made a good bonfire out of them; then I stripped and rubbed down, and put on the dry socks that I always carried slung on my chest, under my shirt. Harris, of course, thought he knew better — laughed at me for a tenderfoot, and hung round without changing or drying his socks; but before we'd gone a mile he was down on his back in the snow howling that his feet were frozen.

Well, I rolled him on to the toboggan and got him back to camp somehow. Then I stripped his legs, and put him in a big chair and lashed him in, so that he couldn't move hand or foot. Then I got a basin of coal-oil and put his feet in it to draw the frost, and of cousre that was absolute agony. After that we got him into bed and chafed his feet with snow. The left foot responded and gradually got the life back into it, but the right foot, from the knuckles of the toes down, and the butt of the heel, was solid. I dressed it for days, but one morning when I was dressing it the skin of the toes came right off like a glove, leaving the purplish decayed flesh behind. And an awful stink! McQuaide and some of the old hands talked the thing over and decided that someone must cut the toes off, or he would die of gangrene, but who would do it? Of course, nobody; so in the end it came back on me.

Somebody had a hack-saw, and we sharpened up some knives and got hold of some sewing-silk, and I got Harris' permission in writing — signed and witnessed. Then I proceeded. McQuaide advised us to look out for the arteries, and when a great spout of blood came two men were told to seize the worm with callipers, pull her out, and tie her with a bit of silk. I allowed enough skin to turn over and sewed it all up, and then we had to cut out the butt of the heel and scrape all round to remove the gangrene. I don't know how long we were at it, but it seemed long enough for a lifetime. (Graham, The Golden Grindstone, *pp. 168-169).*

Friday, March 17, 1899

Waked up at 6 a.m. by McGinnis, calling and informing us that the creek where we are camped appeared to be overflowing where our toboggans were lying. We got up without loss of time and found the information to be correct. Both packages of tea were in the water and several other articles of less importance. The overflow will probably be the cause of another delay. 7 p.m.: could not leave the camp today so we made the best of the time by drying wet goods and making an overland trail to get out to the good ice. If possible we will try to move tomorrow 1½ miles, to where the Gecks are camped.

Saturday, March 18, 1899

Today we put in probably one of the hardest day's work since we left Wind City. We cannot get out of the infernal hole we are in without a long portage, and today we began the work of hauling our cache here, over the trail made yesterday. We made four trips, of one mile each, Henry drawing our loads from the end of the portage to the cache ½ mile farther on. The portage is by long odds the worst we have yet worked on — "up hill and down dale" and one continuous succession of cahots [French for shocks, jolts or bumps]. Will probably move camp tomorrow.

Sunday, March 19, 1899

Moved camp today 1½ miles and are now out of the "infernal hole". Began work about 9 a.m. Made one load to the end of the portage and one through to the camp. Finished about 3:30 p.m. The work was very hard but it is over now, and I hope that it was necessary (which is doubtful) to make up for the task performed. Four parties are camped here: Gecks, Peacock & Co., Craigie and ourselves.

Monday, March 20, 1899

Made two loads today to cache No. 17 and tomorrow we expect to move camp. We intend to make a move of 8 miles if possible. The work today was hard, although an improvement on yesterday and Saturday. The wind is again from the north and is driving the snow off the ice. Our ice creepers hold us alright, but are very severe on the feet. Judge Morse, Merritt and Johnson returned from the pass. They report the distance from this camp as 42 miles. They saw the Whyte-Sennett party about six miles down the other side.

Tuesday, March 21, 1899

Broke camp this morning at 8:40 and reached camp no. 13 at 10:55 a.m. Distance 6½ miles. Gecks are camped here too. On arriving here we found two of the Putnam party just arriving from their camp some 6 or 7 miles up, and they informed us that there was no suitable camping place beyond this point, inside of 3½ or 4 miles. This would make too long a camp to move, so we decided to put up here. Had camp made by 12 a.m. and after dinner went down to the cache for loads. It was well we did so as we found an overflow had just reached the cache. We moved it over to the gravel bar. Unless prevented by water we expect to have all the supplies here by tomorrow night.

This a most remarkable river — the water is continually bursting through in the most unexpected places — today in one place, tomorrow in another. Fortunately it only requires a short time to freeze these floodings. This afternoon we had to wade through four inches of water.

Wednesday, March 22, 1899

Finished bringing up all our goods to this place, cache no. 18. On arriving at this cache this morning we found yesterday's overflow frozen over, but a fresh one rapidly extending over the same place. After some little trouble we found a way round the water and succeeded in bringing everything away in one trip — some of the loads ran as high as 600 pounds. It was very stormy but fortunately we had the wind in our backs on the return trip.

Thursday, March 23, 1899

Up early this morning and left at 8 a.m. with loads for the next cache, no. 19. We intended making two trips, about 4 miles, but found the ice so good that we practically took all in one trip, and instead of going 4 miles we went up to Putnam's camp, 6½ miles. The loads were very unevenly divided — mine being one of the smallest.

We intend moving camp tomorrow and will probably try to move to a point 4 miles above Putnam's — in all 10½.

Although we have had no success with our rifles, not being favored like most of the parties with opportunities to shoot, we have had an abundance of fresh meat this past month. The Indians have provided us with a great deal of meat, and we bought three carcases from the Gecks at five dollars a carcase. The surrounding country seems to be overrun with Cariboo, but we have not felt disposed to use any of our time hunting. We carry our arms most of the time, and hope they prove of value to us.

Friday, March 24, 1899

Broke camp at 9:50 a.m. and reached camp no. 15 at 1:20 p.m. About ¾ of the trail was good; the remainder was over snow hillocks and at times the hauling was very heavy work. Henry and myself hauled loads left over from our cache yesterday. It was 4 p.m. before we had our camp made; this was owing to the load with the tent arriving late. It is many a day since I felt so tired. Do not think that there is much nourishment in cariboo meat. Our meals for some time now have consisted of either boiled or roasted meat and one bun each.

This week proved our best so far but we have worked very hard and intend resting tomorrow.

Len Geck pointed out this afternoon the point where the pass is and it is a great relief to know that the much longed-for point is drawing much closer and actually in view. We have yet about 21 miles to travel before we reach it.

Sunday, March 26, 1899

Did nothing today in the hauling line, my only work being to get in some fire wood.

We are now camped within three miles of "Three Rivers" and hope by tomorrow night to have all our supplies here too. Our next cache will probably be at Three Rivers, and the work on this part will be somewhat hard as we have to haul over three miles of snow trail.

From Three Rivers to the pass is 19 miles and this is our last stage on this side of the "divide". We cannot tell, however, how far we will have to travel on the other side yet; everything depends on how far we have to go to reach navigable water.

The weather is now moderating considerably, although the winds still keep up and in spite of the milder temperature are hard to face.

Monday, March 27, 1899

Up at 6 a.m. and started for the lower cache at 7 a.m. We made an early start in order to avoid the mid-day overflows. Got back at 12:30. Brought up 525 pounds, but left about 200 pounds 1½ miles below camp, and went down this afternoon for same. All loads were reduced at this point owing to the trail being very bad in this section. Distance covered today, 15 miles. This work is beginning to tell on our party and the sooner it is over the better. Man was never intended by the Designer of the Universe for a draught animal. If He had intended it so it is more than possible he would have planned us to move on all fours.

Tuesday, March 28, 1899

Made a load this morning to cache no. 22 and found the trail one of the worst we have passed over. When we returned we found Judge Morse had arrived, and after dinner Millette informed us that he had arranged to travel with the Judge from this point, so instead of making a load this afternoon we remained in camp and arranged settlement with Millette.* I am glad to say that the settlement is very satisfactory and was arrived at very speedily. Personally, I am very sorry to part with Joe as we have agreed very well. The Judge returns tomorrow to Bear River and Joe will await his return; they will then rush through and travel with us.

Editor's note: Millette apparently joined McAdam's party in July of 1898. The first mention made of him is on July 13; sometime later McAdam states that Millette's canoe was swamped and lost. It seems that Millette then joined McAdam's party and they gave him the use of a canvas canoe for his goods. Little else is known about Millette.

Wednesday, March 29, 1899

Made two trips today to cache no. 22, making a total of 14 miles. Used McGinnis's toboggan this afternoon, and found it a great improvement on mine. Expect to move camp tomorrow about 5 miles and then bring up our goods to the edge of the ice. Will be glad when we are over this part of the trail.

Thursday, March 30, 1899: Three Rivers

Broke camp at 8:20 a.m. and reached camp no. 16 at 10:10 a.m. Distance 4½ miles. This short move was made owing to the bar and our having to dispense with the iron shoeing on the toboggans while crossing it. Cache no. 22 is one mile below and we will move it, and the one load still at cache no. 21, to the ice ¾ of a mile above. When this is done we will put the shoeing on the toboggans again and move camp to where the Gecks and Putnams are now, about 4 miles from here. We are all very tired today; in fact, almost "played out." What can the matter be? Is it the cariboo meat we have been living on? We all think it is, as it does not appear to satisfy.

Millette left us today — breakfast being his last meal. I miss him a good deal and feel sorry that it was necessary for him to leave us.

Friday, March 31, 1899

Made two loads today, one between caches no. 21 (last camp) and no. 23; and one between nos. 22 and 23. Total distance 14 miles. Had a good dinner of bacon and beans and feel much better. The days are lengthening out very rapidly. We had our supper this evening by daylight.

Tomorrow we make the first move on the last stage. We are now about 17 miles from the pass, and as we have good ice to travel on most of the way, we hope by the end of next week to reach the summit.

Saturday, April 1, 1899: All Fools Day!

Broke camp at 8:30 a.m. and reached camp no. 17 at 10:30 a.m. This is another short move — only 4½ miles — but from here we expect longer moves till the finish. The "Summit" mountain is now close by, but we have quite a jaunt around it to reach the "pass' — about 13 miles.

This afternoon we hauled up one load each, from the lower cache. We attempted to haul the whole business but only succeeded in drawing loads about ¼ to ½ mile. My load was 650 pounds. Brought through 340 pounds and found the load quite heavy enough.

We suspect tampering with our cache. Andrew was the first to notice it. Our medicine box was opened yesterday and most of our brandy was taken. The loss is very annoying as the spirits were brought as a medicine, and we fear that men who would rob us of one thing would not hesitate to steal our grub.

Sunday, April 2, 1899

We worked this morning in order to get all our supplies here, but are resting this afternoon. Were troubled this morning with overflows and were compelled to wade through water for quite a distance. Attended to a few necessary repairs. The ice plays havoc with footwear.

I am trying to keep hopeful, but as we draw near the gold country I find myself less sanguine of the final result. Our provisions are rapidly disappearing and how we are to replenish our larder is becoming a serious question. At the present time we have only 500 pounds of flour and about 175 pounds of bacon — enough for about 3 or 4 months. It is a long time since I came to the conclusion that our trip has been a big bungle, and have decided that should we be fortunate enough to "strike", I will take good care to see that our provision list is more liberally attended to.* The trip so far has cost us much more than most of the parties here, and in many cases they are better provided for than we are.

Editor's note: "big bungle" is again a reference to McAdam's dissatisfaction with some of his partners and, more specifically it seems, with the leadership. For although one has difficulty, when reading the diary, in determining who was the leader, we know from newspaper sources that the party was organized by Charles Maltby. Perhaps the fact that he is mentioned so seldom is indication that Maltby was not a forceful leader; in any event it seems quite certain that McAdam was not impressed by his organizational or leadership abilities.

Monday, April 3, 1899

We moved camp today a mile and a half — another miserably small advance, but it cannot be helped. We began work this morning by hauling a load to this point where we found the Peacock party (they moved camp this morning too) blocked by an overflow. We anticipated this trouble and came prepared to make a camp here if necessary. We therefore set to work and cleared a camp ground before we returned to dinner. Immediately after dinner we broke camp and moved up, and after went back to the cache and brought up everything. Between here and the last camp there is bad piece of snow trail about ¾ of a mile long. We hope to find the overflow sufficiently frozen by morning to admit of our moving the cache tomorrow. There appears to be good ice ahead of us for some distance.

Tuesday, April 4, 1899

Up at five a.m. Breakfast 5:40. Began hauling at 6 a.m. and by 9 had made two loads to cache no. 26 — 1¼ miles above camp. At 9:20 we broke camp and moved to camp no. 19 — 3½ miles — reaching there at 10:20. This is the best morning's work we have yet done. Fortunately yesterday's overflow was frozen, and by starting early this morning we almost entirely avoided today's, which was spreading rapidly when we came up with our camp outfit. We had to pass over a few yards of water. There are three camp places here. The Peacock party cached here this morning, but have gone ahead with their camp outfit.

This afternoon we brought up goods from cache no. 26 to camp. Mileage for the day: 15 miles.

Wednesday, April 5, 1899

Made one load this morning to cache no. 28 — distance 5 miles. Met the Peacock party coming down to their cache and they informed us that the next camp is 7 miles, instead of 5 miles as we understood. They also informed us that the pass is 3 miles from the next camp, but that the different parties cache one mile beyond. The trail this morning was poor for 2 miles; the remaining 3 miles was all ice and very good.

Made two trips this afternoon, but did not go to cache no. 28; it was too far, but made another cache (#29) at the end of the bad part of the trail.

Mileage today 19 miles. We are all very tired tonight and will sleep well. Tomorrow we have a good day's work before us.

Thursday, April 6, 1899

Broke camp at 7:45 a.m. and reached our 20th and last camp this side of the "divide" at 11 a.m. Distance 7 miles. It was a long and fatiguing haul, and we were glad when we reached camp. Between the two caches we drew 100 pounds extra. What a relief it is to know that our next move will carry us over to the other side, and that this horse work is almost at an end. We understand that from here to the pass — 3 miles — the trail is very bad, ending in water almost to our knees (being part of the performance).

This afternoon we made one trip to cache no. 28.

Tomorrow we have three loads to make, one to cache 29 — 4¾ miles down — and two to cache 28 — 2 miles down.

Mileage today: 11 miles.

Friday, April 7, 1899

This morning we went down to the lower cache and brought up all there to the upper cache. Our loads averaged 340 pounds. From the latter point we brought through 180 pound loads — the trail at this end being only fair.

We attempted to draw the balance of cache 28 in one trip this afternoon — distance 2 miles — but found it necessary to reduce the loads at bad places. We saved about 1½ miles.

We are now, bag and baggage, 3 miles from the Summit and begin tomorrow to move our supplies to the last cache on this "side".

We have had a little fresh snow the past two days, the first for a long time, and it made the hauling very hard work. Often when very much fatigued those two fine songs, "Tired" and "Home, Sweet Home," come to mind with great force, and remind me that rest is soon to follow and also that the object of all this hard work is to provide myself with a little place, "be it ever so humble."

Saturday, April 8, 1899

Made two trips this morning to cache no. 31, and intended making two this afternoon, but succeeded in hauling all that remained after the morning's work in one trip. The loads were heavy considering the poor trail — mine was 260 pounds. We had about a 100 yards of water to go through. It was not deep, still sufficiently so to wet my feet and they were wet all day.

When we arrived at the cache with our afternoon load we decided to lighten our loads and continue on to the Summit. We took through 200 pounds and made a cache (no. 32) at the Summit. So we have at last seen the "divide." We did not go sufficiently far to see the beginning of the drop on the other side, which we understand is considerable, but if it is anything like the slope we have had to climb on this side, our work will be much lighter when we begin the descent.

Andrew and Henry shot about 20 ptarmigan yesterday afternoon and this morning.

Sunday, April 9, 1899

We are observing today [Sunday] as a day of rest so far as travelling is concerned. Henry and Andrew have gone out to see if they can get us a little moose meat, and I intended trying for a mess of trout, but it turned cold and blustering during the night and I have changed my mind. The Hopkins party killed about 150 trout a week or so ago, about 2 miles down in a small channel not frozen over. They were very small.

Joe and Judge Morse have not caught up to us yet. What is the matter? We left Joe the 30th of March and he expected the Judge to arrive on Sunday the 2nd and to catch up to us by the 4th; here it is the 9th and they have not arrived yet.

Monday, April 10, 1899

"The Pass"

At last we are camped at the "pass" with all our supplies. We are not yet through with this slavish work, however, but are more than satisfied to know that the end is practically in sight. It will probably take us about 10 days to reach our last camp, which we must make far enough down to ensure navigable water. We expect to find all the parties ahead of us camped about 15 miles down the Stewart River at another point called Three Rivers.

We broke camp this morning at 8:50 and intended moving about 5 miles — to the other side of the pass — but once again we were disappointed. The storm that began yesterday morning is still to the fore and the trail is full of snow. We found the work this morning desperately hard, and were quite satisfied to move 3 miles. We were over 2½ hours covering this distance and it was 2 o'clock before we had dinner. Our camp is two hundred yards from the trail, and we had a job wading and hauling our toboggans through the deep snow to reach it. We had to make a new camp, as ours is the only party so far to camp on the pass. Expected to have found the water below frozen over, but it was worse than ever — the snow holding the flow in check and making it deeper, although more slush than water. As luck would have it, one of the runners of my toboggan broke while in the worst part, and I had to stand and allow the water to penetrate through my mocassins and socks before I could get out.

I have completed a distance table to this point, and extended the same into a total column. Our two caches are about equal distance above and below us, so that our work on Wind River is finished. Will show our work from now till the end of the Winter's work in a separate section. My table shows the distance from Wind City to the Pass as 143½ miles. Dr. Brown's cyclometer measurement shows the distance as 136. I am satisfied with my table, however, and I think if there is any error it is one of shortage.

Mileage to date: with loads 412¾; without loads, 269¼. Total: 682 miles; actual distance travelled, 143½ miles.

Number of working days (counting one day my cook week), 60; average total mileage per day, 11.36 miles; average actual distance per day, 2.39 miles. Greatest distance one day, 20 miles. Greatest actual distance one day (with all supplies), 3½ miles. Average camp move, 6.83 miles.

Tuesday, April 11, 1899

Today we made three trips to cache no. 33 and disposed of cache no. 31. With the exception of about 300 pounds at cache 32, all our goods are now deposited on the banks of the Stewart River. While three of us were making our last loads this afternoon, Henry hauled from cache 32 to 33, leaving only the

300 pounds stated above! We had to break trail the whole way this morning, the storm having completely filled it in with snow, and at times we had trouble finding it. It was uphill work most of the way. The storm, or rather the high wind, continued all day and while the first trip was by far the worst, we had to break considerable parts of the trail the last two trips. The distance covered today — 15 miles — represents one of the hardest days work we have put in since leaving Wind City.

The wind is still holding high carnival, and by tomorrow morning the trail will be filled in again. Fortunately one trip more (with camp outfit) will complete this section. We expect to move camp tomorrow.

Today we finished our beans, and must now use peas as a substitute. We are all sorry they are finished as they undoubtedly were the best food of any for this country.*

*Editor's note: All prospectors agreed that beans were indispensable; Ogilvie recommended that the requirement for a year's travel for one man was 120 pounds of beans, one of the largest items on his food list (save flour, sugar and bacon).

Wednesday, April 12, 1899

Stewart River (or Tributary)

We broke camp this morning at 8:30 and arrived at this camp (32) at 12:15 p.m. — or 2 miles over the "height of land" and 3½ miles down the Stewart River — in all a move of 5½ miles. At last we are on one of the Yukon feeders and one that is supposed to be very rich. Unfortunately, however, we must not feel too certain about our position. The information that this is a branch of the Stewart River we received from the Indians — is the information correct? We hope it is, as it means a great deal to us.*

Our camp is pitched in a very pretty piece of scenery. The bush is quite heavy and the willows and alders much heavier than we have seen for some time.

*Editor's note: As stated previously, none of the men were very sure of just where they were. Nor was this unreasonable since much of that country was unexplored and remained so until men like Charles Camsell did so. There were no maps (at least no detailed maps) and all miners relied solely on either the advice of the Indians or Hudson's Bay men. That men did indeed get lost is indicated by an entry in R. H. S. Cresswell's diary which states: "Three miners turned up on their way down the Peel from Dawson, thinking they were on the Porcupine until we told them of their error. They are from Seattle. . . . Captain Parker from London and four others came down the Peel, also mistaking it for the Porcupine." (Alaska Sportsman *[November, 1953], p. 35).*

Thursday, April 13, 1899

Made three trips today and began our cache here. Had to go to cache 32 this morning to bring up the 300 pounds left there. Found the water overflowing at its highest point and threatening to cut us off, so before returning to dinner we moved all the goods (caches 32 and 33) down 1½ miles and brought through loads averaging 175 to 180 pounds. The trail from here to the ice (2 miles) is very bad and will require us to make two loads tomorrow. In the afternoon we will begin moving farther down, but have no information as to the condition of the trail.

We are now fairly started, moving down stream, but up or down makes very little difference as far as the work is concerned. For the first mile or so we had a heavy down grade and had to hold our toboggans back, but it was an ice trail and we fear too good for us to count on much of it.

This evening we had an apricot pie, a good big one to celebrate the "Passover."*

Henry and Andrew killed 20 ptarmigan today.

Editor's note: One wonders whether McAdam is offering us a pun. Are they celebrating the religious event (the time of year is certainly right for it) or the fact that they have "passed over" the divide. Perhaps both.

Friday, April 14, 1899

We succeeded in bringing up cache no. 34 in one load — about 250 pounds each — it's saved one trip and made up for the hard pull. We did not leave loads at cache 35, but continued on to a point 2 miles below camp.* This afternoon we moved cache here to the same place as this morning (cache 36). We made one trip only, but had to make two hauls over short sections, where the trail was bad. Our loads were about 325 pounds each. Most of the trail for the next 2 miles is mostly good ice. There is some water but we had little difficulty in getting around it. There would be a great difference in the distance table if the trail was straight occasionally, but such is not the case; it is one continuous succession of bends and twists.

We have had no news from parties behind us for two weeks, and we have no information whatsoever as to where the parties ahead of us are.

Tomorrow we move camp again and will probably work on Sunday as the season is advancing rapidly and we must keep at it till we arrive at the end of the Winter's work.

The scenery around here is beautiful, especially in the evening after sunset. There appears to be twilight here, or a light that resembles it, as it is quite light for two hours before sunrise and after sunset. The sun shows a rapid advance toward the North, morning and evening.

Henry killed 14 ptarmigan today.

*Editor's note: The terms "above" and "below" may be slightly confusing at this point, after having been reading them so long in an opposite way. Coming up Wind River, "above" would mean "in advance of" the camp and "below" would mean a trip back to a cache. Now that the party is going down river (the Stewart), "above" and "below" have reversed their meanings. To add to our confusion, McAdam sometimes confuses the words himself.

Saturday, April 15, 1899

Broke camp at 8:40 a.m. and reached camp no. 23 at 12:15 p.m. For two miles — up to our cache — we found the trail fairly good, but from that point to camp it was about as bad as it could be. We had to break trail for over three miles, and a trail that, at its best, must have been very bad. My load was heavy (200 pounds) for such work, and I was quite satisfied to stop when we did, although it would have been much more satisfactory could we have made two miles more. We had to build a new camp place, and had to shovel out a hole four feet deep.

On the way I was tempted to try my luck with my rifle at a ptarmigan and succeeded in breaking its neck. Also tried my hand with the shotgun and wounded my bird, but he got away. Ptarmigan (white partridge) are very plentiful. We see a great many and are having some very good meals of them.

It is surprising that this country should have any bird life whatever during the winter months since it is so cold, and yet we have had quite a lot of our feathered friends with us all winter. The Whisky-jack, or "Camp robber", we see every day around our camp. They are quite tame and come quite close to our tent and pick up scraps thrown out. It is a bird about the size of a robin, of dirty white and light blue plumage. Then there is a small bird, white and gray, with dark gray pencilling and a little red on the head. I do not know the Chickadee, but judge by its notes that it is this bird.

Distance 5 miles.

Sunday, April 16, 1899

Up about 7:00 a.m. Had breakfast at 7:30. Had a visit from Millette just after our morning meal. He and Judge and Dad Brown have arrived at our last camp 5 miles up, but their caches are still above. The Hamilton party, Joe said, would probably reach the same camp tomorrow. We are not surprised at Joe and the Judge being so near, but were a little surprised to hear about the other parties being so close.* Today made three hauls. The morning trip through to the cache, ¾ of a mile beyond our tent. In the afternoon we made two partial trips. Instead of hauling one load directly to the cache, as in the morning, we brought tomorrow's load up two miles and then went back and brought all that remained to camp, so that we have supplies at three points. The mileage for today is much more than we anticipated doing when we began work this morning — 17½ miles — but now that it is done we feel satisfied with "that tired feeling," although we unfortunately omitted bringing any of Dr. Williams Pink Pills with us.

My eyes have been troubling me of late; snow blindness, I suppose. Two days ago at noon I suffered considerably and have used smoked glasses since. Four of us have been troubled of late.

We are hoping that by next Sunday we will be through with this work, but of course cannot say [for sure].

Editor's note: If the "Hamilton party" to which Joe refers is that consisting of Cresswell, Tallman and Skynner (A. D. Stewart had died), then he is certainly wrong in saying they were close behind. According to Cresswell's diary, the party is still at its winter camp and did not reach the divide until August.

Monday, April 17, 1899

Made two trips today. Went down this morning and brought up yesterday afternoon's first load which we had left one mile below camp and in the afternoon took through our camp load and when passing cache 37 we added to our loads, disposing of it [cache 37]. Everything is now at cache 38, about 2½ miles from here, where there is an old camp. About six parties appear to have camped here at the same time. We intended going farther, but were blocked by an overflow that extended across the river. At one point we had to open a trail, through deep snow along the bank and draw half loads across. We had to wear snowshoes to do so as the snow was very soft and there was about four inches of water at the bottom. My footwear was soaking wet all day and of course my feet were very cold. Tried my hand with the shotgun today and brought down three ptarmigan. Missed one.

The weather today was very warm, and for the first time this Spring the sun showed visible effects on the snow. On our way back the wind turned round to the North and it turned quite cold.

Intend making an early start tomorrow morning and hope to find the overflows frozen.

Tuesday, April 18, 1899

Broke camp at 5:45 a.m. Charlie, Andrew and myself did not come through to camp with our outfit, but only 5 miles where we dropped our loads; Plen and Henry brought our loads through to camp. We then returned to the cache, 2½ miles back, and brought up 400 pound loads to camp and in the afternoon continued with the same loads to cache 39, three miles beyond camp. Distance table shows full camp move of 7 miles; in order to keep the actual mileage complete, but in order to keep the table correct, I have reduced the cache move — round trip 11 miles, instead of 15 being the correct mileage for round trip between caches.

Found very little water in the early morning, but when returning with our loads of supplies we had to wade through 4 inches of water in places. We intended returning to our upper cache in the afternoon but could not owing to the water, so we made use of the afternoon in taking another load farther on.

The surrounding country appears to be changing rapidly. This afternoon we passed several of the highest hills clothed to the top with timber. On the Wind River most of the hills had sharp peaks; on this side a great many have rounded tops. For sometime past we have been travelling a good deal to the east, but today we made a big swing to the west. This is encouraging.

We passed through today what appears to be a canyon — about 1½ miles long. When on the other side, we heard of a canyon and hope that this was what the Indians referred to.

Wednesday, April 19, 1899

Today we made a through trip from cache 39 to 40 — 4½ miles above camp to 4½ miles below camp — in all 18 miles. We stopped on the way through at camp for dinner. On the way from the upper cache to camp we passed through fully 2½ miles of water, varying from 1 to 5 inches deep. It was by far the worst trail so far as water is concerned, that we have yet had to pass over. Of course our footwear was thoroughly soaked and the sensation of wading through ice cold water, while refreshing, was far from comfortable. The afternoon trip was much more comfortable, and we went 1½ miles below the cache (39) made yesterday afternoon to a large camp ground where probably 5 or 6 parties have camped. On a sign left there we learned the joyable [sic] news that we have only 14 miles to go beyond that camp to reach "the large river and hot springs," and that the trail was good, and also that Dr. Brown and the Bay City party (the

Swedes) were there building boats. What a relief it is to know something definite about "the beyond." Up till the present we have been in complete darkness as to how far we had to go down this river; now that miserable uncertainty has disappeared and this work will be completed within a week.

Today Constant Segard, better known as Francis, paid us a visit, with the object of trying to join our party. He has 375 pounds of flour, and his bedding, but nothing else. At first we thought of admitting him as a travelling companion only, but on fully considering the matter we decided to admit him as a full partner. He cannot speak English although he understands a good deal of our language. He is a very handy man and a good worker, and while it will be an advantage to him to join us, there are advantages that we will gain by having him. The flour that he throws in with our supplies is a "God find," and makes the Summer's work more hopeful.

Thursday, April 20, 1899

Up at 4:20 a.m. Breakfast at 5 and at 6:45 Andrew and myself started off with part of the camp outfit for camp no. 25 — distance 4½ miles. The others followed later. We started first in order to get our choice of camping places. We chose one yesterday and partially fixed it, and were determined to have it at the expense of rising a couple of hours earlier. Francis brought up 250 pounds yesterday and we divided it amongst us, and brought it through with our camp outfit. He went back 4½ miles for the balance of his possessions. After dinner we brought all of cache 39 to cache 40.

Judge Morse and Millette are here now and will probably go ahead of us as they have only two loads, while we have three. There is another small party here: Rennsellar, Bob Onslow and Johnson. Went out this afternoon ptarmigan hunting with Andrew. We killed three; Andrew killed two. There are not many in this neighbourhood.

Friday, April 21, 1899

Made two trips today to cache no. 41. All our supplies are now four miles ahead of us. The trail was very good for about 2½ miles; the rest was very bad. My morning load was 300 pounds and the afternoon load about 275 pounds. The work was not very heavy where the trail was good, but in the bad parts it was and particularly in those places where our loads showed a very strong desire to roll over, and which they very often succeeded in doing.

Tomorrow will move camp 7 miles midway between this point and the finish.

Saturday, April 22, 1899

Broke camp at 8 a.m. and reached camp no. 26 at 12 a.m. Distance 7½ miles. The trail was very heavy owing to a light snow fall during the night. The snow was very soft and acted as a sort of glue. The last two miles were practically all water and up to date the worst piece of water trail we have yet passed through. The water was not as deep as some we have passed through, but the stretches were so long that at times we thought our feet would freeze before we could reach the dry places. We were delayed about half an hour on the way owing to some ptarmigan appearing on the scene. I succeeded in killing four and wounding two. The latter got away before we could reach them. The snow was too deep to follow without snowshoes. We intended bringing a load down this afternoon from the cache, but have changed our minds owing to the bad trail.

Sunday, April 23, 1899

Up at 4:30 a.m. Breakfast at 5 a.m. Left for cache at 5:30. After going a short distance and finding that the trail was very bad — the overflows not having frozen — I returned to the camp and borrowed a pair of rubber boots (mine were up at the cache) and went back. Drew two loads to the edge of the water, then brought one over the water and returned for the other. Brought last load through to the camp, and Andrew brought the first load. Loads 325 and 340 pounds. Wore my miner's boots after the trip up, and while they leaked I found them much more comfortable wading in ice-cold water than moccasins. Everything is here now.

This afternoon it rained quite heavily for about three hours.

Monday, April 24, 1899

We are not doing anything today in the moving line. The rain has interfered considerably with our work by making much worse a trail that was already bad. We may be delayed here sometime. Henry, Millette and Lyman Brown left this morning, about 8 a.m., to pay a visit to the people ahead of us (about 6 or 7 miles) and to learn something about the trail we have still to go over, and also to look up good camp grounds. We want to get close to good timber for building our boat. Henry returned about 6 p.m. and reported all well ahead. The information given on the sign at the camp behind, that the "big river and hot springs were 14 miles down" was not altogether correct. The distance is correct for the hot springs but the "big river" is 10 miles farther down. The Gecks and Putnams have gone down to the "big river", all the rest are here in camp at the hot springs and have several boats built. We were looking forward to a good trail, but on this point we are to be disappointed, as it is very bad.

Tuesday, April 25, 1899

Up at 3:30 a.m. Breakfast at 4; we began hauling our cache forward at 5 a.m. First load taken down 1¾ miles and the second load 3½ miles. At 11:30 a.m. had dinner and at 1:20 p.m. we left with our camp outfit. After four hours of hard work we reached a point just above our 3½ mile cache and made camp. The trail was much worse than in the morning, the sun having played mischief with it. The work is becoming much harder as the season advances and it is well we are near the end.

Wednesday, April 26, 1899

Up at 4 a.m. and left at 4:40 for the loads above; reached camp on our way through at 7:30; had some beef tea; after we took loads 1½ miles down. We then returned and took the cache here to same place. We are resting this afternoon, intending to make a very early start tomorrow morning for our Spring camp.

Thursday, April 27, 1899

Broke camp at 4:30 a.m. and reached the "ship-yard" camp at 6 a.m. Thank heavens! Our tent is at last pitched at the point where tobogganing ceases. We intended having all our supplies here too, but by the time we had our camp made the sun was high and part of the trail impassable. It is only two miles from here to the cache and we will go tomorrow and end this business. Our camp is pitched on a high bluff.

Friday, April 28, 1899

"It is finished"

This morning we completed the work we began last January — hauling toboggans, and if ever men earned a good rest, we have. We are now in the gold country (?). It has taken us nearly fourteen months to reach this place, and the next few months will tell what reward we are to have, as a company. We are all

Indians photographed tracking the Hudson's Bay Company's fur boats up the rapids on the Athabasca River.

Members of the McAdam party are photographed at one of their caches.

Snowed-in shacks at Wind City, winter of 1898-99

This drawing of George Mitchell's log cabin at Wind City was taken from The Golden Grindstone.

Gold washing with a grizzley. McAdam was working on a similar grizzley at Wind City.

These Indian guides were photographed by McAdam.

Winter lodges of the Kutchin Indians. This drawing is from A. H. Murray's Journal to the Yukon, 1847-48; *it closely approximates McAdam's description.*

—Provincial Archives of Alberta

Dawson City, 1898

Peter and Neal: the Wind City mail carriers

This was McAdam's first home in Dawson City.

A trading store at Dawson City at the turn of the century

One of the more famous residents of Dawson City — Robert Service

hopeful, and intend working hard for success. Washing and general cleanup is now the order of the day.

Editor's note: It is now 415 days since McAdam and his partners have left the city of Montreal. All but about a dozen of these days have been spent in paddling, tracking and hauling — a long wilderness tramp by any standard.

Sunday, May 7, 1899

Last night I succeeded in getting this book to continue my diary. Joe White was kind enough to give it to me.*

*Editor's note: with his entry of April 28, McAdam had completely used up the second of his small notebooks. As of May 7 the diary is contained in a larger account book and it is to this which he refers. Joe White deserves our thanks also, for without him we would not be able to enjoy the conclusion of McAdam's adventure. The entry which follows fills in the details for the 29th and 30th of April to May 7, 1899.

On the former date [April 29] we had a general cleanup — a bath and change of clothes. We were very much in need of both and felt very much more comfortable after the change. On the 30th Charlie, Andrew and myself left with a light fishing outfit for the chain of lakes, in back of this point, on a hunting and fishing expedition. We returned on the 4th disgusted at our luck, not having fired a shot and with only three fish (grey trout, about 1½ pounds each) to our credit. Going out we crossed the hills in back of us, but found the trail so bad that we took the other trail, via the lakes, creeks and river, when coming back: the former distance was 8½ miles; the latter about 10½ miles. While away we camped beside Dad Brown, Waterman and McQuaide. As usual, Dad Brown's luck followed him, and on the morning after their arrival two moose — a cow and calf — came on to the lake, about 200 yards from their tent, and stood till killed. Quite a number of men were back trying to secure a few cariboo or moose, but lately this section gave very few opportunities to the hunter to add meat to his larder. The Swedes and other earlier parties to arrive here appear to have scared the game away. While on the Wind River we saw signs of enormous herds, but nothing in comparison with what we saw on the lakes — signs of both moose and cariboo. The whole region was tramped down like a barnyard. A few were killed by the more fortunate during the time we were back, but not many. Frank Sennett and Hopkins, however, made a very good showing, about 4 miles from where we were camped — they "bunched" a lot of cariboo and got 14 of them. We tried our hand at fishing and while the showing was miserable, still we did succeed! We cut three holes in the ice and sank five baits; in three days we caught three trout.

The Swedes claim to have caught trout as high as 10 pounds and Fred Payzant some four pounds. Francis paid us a visit Thursday morning; that same morning we broke camp at 8:30 a.m. and reached him at 4 p.m. We stopped about noon for about two hours, and had something to eat.

During our absence from camp Henry and Francis felled and squared logs for a boat and on Friday we brought them down to the river in front of the camp. Some of them were high up on the hill back of us and it required considerable hard work to get them out; consequently, while the work was something new, I cannot say it afforded any of us pleasure. On Saturday, the 6th, we spent the morning hauling the logs into position under the saw pit and in the afternoon helped to bring in a week's firewood.

We rested all day today (7th), Sunday.

Monday, May 8, 1899

Today Charlie and I went down the river to pick gum for our boat. We left at 8 a.m. and returned at 3:45 p.m. We carried rifles in the hope of killing a stray moose or cariboo, but to no purpose. We collected 7 or 8 pounds of gum. The river is breaking up rapidly and consequently travelling on it is very bad. The day was miserable — a heavy damp snow falling most of the day. Henry and Andrew sawed one log on Saturday and began the second this morning, but were compelled to stop work owing to the weather.

We made an unexpected discovery today. In a bag supposed to contain two 50 pound sacks of flour, one of the sacks contained about 35 or 40 pounds of sugar. Had we lots of flour on hand, the discovery would have been a pleasant surprise, but unfortunately this is not the case. It is quite possible, however, that we may be able to exchange the sugar for flour or something else that is more necessary. We had sugar in our tea tonight — the first time for many months.

The weather is becoming much milder, and each day shows a higher registration on the thermometer. The snow is melting quite rapidly and the small mountain streams are running freely.

The days are lengthening out — daylight lasting now from about 2:30 a.m. till 9:30 p.m.

Tuesday, May 9, 1899

Up at 4 a.m. and left at 5 a.m. with Charlie on another gum-collecting expedition. We succeeded in collecting about 6 pounds. We now have about 20 pounds, which will probably be more than sufficient. (Charlie and Andrew brought some back with them from the lakes.) We carried rifles again, with the usual luck; saw signs — fresh tracks — on our way back, but that was all. Our luck will probably turn some day. A moose was killed today about two miles from camp, by one of the Swedes. I am very tired tonight; the walking was desperately bad, every step we sank to our knees, and as the snow was heavy and wet, returned with damp feet. Wore my miner's boots and although I found them heavy (6 pounds), I find them much more comfortable and warm when my feet are wet than moccasins.

Wednesday, May 10, 1899

Remained in camp all today. Did some darning and general repairs, and set my clothes to soak overnight. Anticipate quite a job washing them and hope they do not go into rags under the operation.

Today we exchanged the 20 pounds of sugar for 40 pounds of beans.

Thursday, May 11, 1899

Spent the morning washing my clothes. They held together very well and they will probably stand a little more wear and tear.

Made another exchange today. Gave Joe White and Hopkins 3 pounds of sugar and 3 pounds of cocoa for a cariboo. We are turning the sugar to good account. We weighed the sugar as we found it 36 pounds and have now made the value of 50 pounds of flour out of it, and have still a little left for ourselves.

We had a first class meal tonight. We had all we could eat of cariboo steak and it was undoubtedly the finest meat I have tasted since we came into the country.

Friday, May 12, 1899

Today we worked for awhile bringing in firewood — enough to last us while we stay here. We have to go quite a distance for it, and as the trails are bad we want to get it in while we can. Began today making the floats for nets. Will complete the job tomorrow.

Saturday, May 13, 1899

Did not do much today. Made floats for our two nets, and a patterns sinker. Henry and Andrew completed whip-sawing lumber for the boat and sundries. They make good lumber. The boat builders begin Monday and expect to have the ship built by Saturday.

Sunday, May 14, 1899

Spent the day quietly. In the afternoon cast sinkers for the net. Went to bed about 9 p.m.

Monday, May 15, 1899

Tested sinkers and floats this morning with the outcome that I had to make a new set of sinkers, the first being too light.

Began sign board for the boat this afternoon: "St. Lawrence of Montreal."

With the exception of the immediate vicinity, the surrounding country presents a winter appearance; all the hills are covered with snow and the river, while it cannot be considered safe, is still ice bound. A few small channels are open, but many of these remain open all winter. Our summer friends, the wild geese and ducks, are arriving daily and our smaller feathered friends, the chickadees, surround our camp in great numbers. We are perfectly satisfied to see all such friends, but unfortunately enemies have also put in an appearance, particularly the dreaded mosquito. Several have been seen of late and yesterday I saw one for the first time this year. For these pests to appear so early we were not prepared, and must now expect to see them increase rapidly, and prepare to protect ourselves. A large variety of the house fly has also put in an appearance.

Tuesday, May 16, 1899

Finished my sign board for the boat today, and carved initials — St. L. — on a number of our tools. In a crowd such as is here at present (85 men) a great deal of borrowing is done, and some way of identifying our belongings is necessary.

Yesterday saw a considerable rise in the river and today it continues rising. We have now running water on this side of the islands (the main river runs on the far side), and it is now probable that it will not be necessary for us to begin our Spring work with a portage from the shipyard to the river.

This evening we put our canvas boat together.

Wednesday, May 17, 1899

Helped Henry all day, planing board for the boat.

The river continues to rise and we have now quite a body of water running in front of our camp.

Thursday, May 18, 1899: Edith's Birthday

Worked part of today planing boards for the boat.

Doc Conley, Ben W. and Bennett left today. They are the first to move, but we do not think they can go very far as the river is only open in places here and there. It is too early for navigation.

Friday, May 19, 1899

Began work this morning on a "grizzly" for washing gold. It will probably require about three days to make it.*

Today Henry and Francis finished planking the boat. This is the heaviest part. We are short of nails of all sizes and cannot get any more.

Word came up this morning that Doc Conley only got down one mile yesterday.

The river continues rising.

Heard first robin this evening and it sent a thrill of pleasure through me.

*Editor's note: Perhaps to best way to define a "grizzly" is to attach the illustration from the Dictionary of Canadianisms *and refer the reader to that excellent book for further amplification. It is perhaps obvious that dirt is shovelled into the box, water poured over it and washed towards the "grizzly head": any gold in the dirt will attach itself to the screen.*

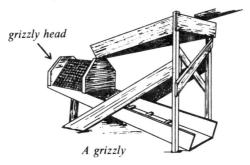

grizzly head

A grizzly

Saturday, May 20, 1899

Worked all day on the "grizzly" — that is, I worked when I could get hold of the tools as I required them, and a part of the bench to work on — the result was a good deal of wasted time and not much work done. The tools and bench were being used by those working on the boat.

Fine weather and the mosquitoes are beginning to get troublesome. We are in for a good time with the pests.

Departures: Fred Dench and McQuaide.

Sunday, May 21, 1899

Worked this morning on the "grizzly" and in the afternoon rested for the best part.

Shortly after dinner the ice began coming down in large quantities and all the citizens set to work to get the boats out of danger; before we succeeded in getting them all out of the water three were badly damaged; Jean Lanonette's, John Rennsaler's and Craigie's. These parties will be delayed some time, but will have time to make repair before it is safe to leave. There is great anxiety on the part of most here to get away as soon as possible, and it is probable that some will leave before it is safe. We hope that those who have already gone are out of danger.

We are to have an apricot pie this evening to celebrate the completion of the boat.

Carved two pipes today for Peck's two brothers, putting on their monograms, with Pecks above [ARCTIC F/P CIRCLE].*

8 p.m. We received news at supper time that the people below were safe.

Another ice jam has just moved down and the sight was grand. The current in front of the camp is running at probably a 7-mile rate.

Editor's note: In a separate notebook McAdam kept a record of the pipes which he engraved. For example, on the 26th of May he notes that he engraved the pipes of C. D. Mills and D. J. McAuliffe, both of the Hamilton party. McAdam also engraved rifle butts and apparently gained a fair reputation for doing so.

Monday, May 22, 1899

Worked all day on the "grizzly" and finished it.

The ice has probably all passed us; that is, all that is coming down. The river is now flowing in the main channel and there is very little water in front of the camp.

Parties are leaving each day and we will soon be alone.

Tuesday, May 23, 1899

Began work today on a rocker, but did very little, spending most of the time hunting for wood.

At last we have succeeded in killing large game. Henry was the lucky man. Shortly before supper Constant noticed two moose crossing the river above camp ·and immediately told Henry and Andrew. Both started off and in about 10 minutes we had one of the animals. The other got away, although Henry claims it was wounded.

Wrote Sis and Linda today. Millette is taking the letters out.

Editor's note: McAdam also kept a separate record of his rifle's produce, entitled "My Rifle's Record":

May 23	Bull Moose	Shot by Henry
May 29	Cow Moose	Andrew and McAdam
May 29	Calf	McAdam
June 2	Cow Moose	McAdam
June 2	Cow Moose	McAdam and Andrew

McAdam commented earlier that the hunting luck of his party was bound to turn, sooner or later; it certainly seems very good at this point.

Wednesday, May 24, 1899: Queen's Birthday

I wonder if my chums are trout fishing today. I hope they are and that they have a spare thought or two for the one far away.*

Worked all day on my rocker and all that is necessary to make for the present is now made.

After supper this evening Henry had a splendid opportunity to kill another moose. He got within range of 100 yards, but failed to bring him down. I saw his last shot and the animal winced, but got away at a good rate. They followed for some distance but, if wounded, the brute had evidently enough life left to get to a distance where it would not be convenient for us to go.

Hopkins, Dad Brown, Joe White and Curran parties, and Joe and Judge [Morse] left today. Only the Hamilton party and ourselves are here now.

*Editor's note: When Canada used to celebrate May 24 as the Queen's Birthday (Queen Victoria), it was traditional, in Eastern Canada at least, to take advantage of the holiday for the season's first major trouting expedition, with prizes being offered for the largest catch, largest trout, etc. Undoubtedly, though, McAdam was in better fishing country than most of his chums would be.

Thursday, May 25, 1899

Did not sleep well last night. In fact my slumbers for two or three nights past have been wretched imitations of sleep. I have felt a little "blue" of late, and do not know whether to blame the want of sleep for the attack or the reverse.

After breakfast this morning I went out to pick gum for caulking the boat; what we picked some time ago was not sufficient. By dinner time we had gathered sufficient, and Henry finished the work. After dinner we launched the boat, with the assistance of the Hamilton party who were kind enough to wait several hours to help us; we then set to work to load and get out.

We finished about six o'clock and then had supper, after which we cast loose and began another stage of our long journey. The Hamilton party left about 2 o'clock and promised to wait for us ten miles down — where Gecks and Putnams camped. We left at 6:45 p.m. and reached the Hamilton camp at 9:15. Distance 10 miles.

After moving about 2½ miles we sighted the wreck of a scow ahead of us and when passing read the name "Maggie": owners Peacock, Barclay, Feltham, Payzant and Crichton. A little farther down we ran ashore and found a bag of dunnage belonging to Feltham. We also saw several boxes and oars. On arriving here we were informed by the Hamilton party, who saw several of the people camped 8 miles below, that the poor fellows had lost everything that they had [except] the clothes on their backs. They got jammed in the ice and had to save their lives by floating on an ice flow to the shore. The Hamilton party picked up a lot of blankets. Had we known that the boat was full of supplies we would have made an attempt to save some and brought same down. The party did not make any attempt to save their goods, but managed to get down to the camp below where the people raised a small quantity of supplies and built them a boat. They are going right through to Dawson.

The trip to this point was exciting, but our boat acted very well. The river is free of ice. We passed through some magnificent scenery. The hills run up 4000 to 5000 feet.

Good Bye Spring City!

Friday, May 26, 1899

A miserable day; rained most of the time and we remained at anchor all day with the Hamiltons. Andrew and Dave Hall went up to the wrecked "Maggie", to try to float her and let her drift down, but their trouble went for nothing, as the water had risen so high it was impossible to reach her from the shore. It seems a pity that something cannot be saved out of the wreck, besides what has been picked up along the shore. There are two good rifles and a shot gun on board. None here can understand why the owners did not make an attempt to save their goods; it seems a case of complete discouragement. Think of what it means: not simply a loss of a few dollars worth of goods, although the loss in dollars is considerable, but eighteen months labour practically lost and at a moment when most required.

Saturday, May 27, 1899

Remained all day at anchor. The morning was miserable, but the afternoon turned out fine and we took advantage of the fine part of the day to dry out the dunnage belonging to Dick Feltham; the Hamiltons had several large blankets to dry, goods also belonging to the "Maggie."

Henry erected a tent-awning for the scow. It will not be necessary for us to go ashore at nights now.

A report from below states that two miles below there is an ice jam or there was two days ago when the report was received. This is one of the reasons why we have not been in a hurry to move.

Are we on the Beaver River, a tributary of the Stewart River? Where are we? This river, whether the Beaver or not, is certainly entitled to that name, as beaver are very numerous here. We went out yesterday to see if we could kill one or two, but it appears to have been one of their days to stop in.

Ducks and geese are plentiful in this neighbourhood and the Gecks killed a swan while camped here.

Sunday, May 28, 1899

Began drifting downstream at 11 a.m. and stopped at 7:10 p.m. We had dinner while floating and supper after we finished the day at 8:30. We calculate the rate of current at 3½ to 4 miles [an hour], and the distance covered in the 7½ hours (we stopped on the way for about 45 minutes) travelling as 30 miles. We passed either two or three streams entering this stream on the left. I am under the impression that we are on a main stream and not some small tributary of the Stewart River. The river for a long piece is fully 150 to 200 yards wide, and as this is the width that Ogilvie states the Stewart is at its mouth, I think that it must be the Stewart itself, although it appears to be even too wide (this high up) to be this river.* In the 30 miles travelled yesterday we passed only two small rapids. The scenery was magnificent, the whole of yesterday's stretch, although during the latter part there was considerable change in the hills, many of them being much lower, with rounded tops and fully clothed with spruce. The highest mountains rise to pointed peaks and are still covered with snow.

The Hamiltons stopped at two points and prospected. The first time on a bar and found nothing, but the second time they found prospects at the mouth of a mountain stream. They went up a short distance, so that the colors evidently came down the stream. Ed Ingraham, the miner of the party, and a man who has done a good deal of work on the Saskatchewan, thinks that the water is too high to do good work, and that we should wait for 10 days or so till the water drops. There is a general desire on the

119

part of both parties to travel together, and it appears to me to be a good plan, although under [?] this desire there appears to be, on the part of some of our company, an eagerness to forge ahead and not give this part of the country a fair showing. It is an easy matter to go downstream to Dawson (if we are on the right river) but we have not travelled the distance we have just to see Dawson, but to get gold and if we are to get gold we must look for it.

Editor's note: McAdam again questions his party's whereabouts, whether, in fact, they are on the right river, but he is not very concerned about the matter because even if it were one of the tributaries of the Stewart it would eventually lead to the Stewart and the Yukon. They were, as we later learn, on the Stewart itself.

The indecision regarding whether or not to stop and prospect was largely due to the fact that most miners felt it best to get to Dawson City as soon as possible and get information about the best places to look for gold. As it turned out, very little gold was taken from this part of Stewart River. See my note for June 13 for a more detailed account of the Stewart River strikes.

Monday, May 29, 1899

Left anchorage at 9:30 a.m. and arrived here (Lansing Creek?) at 10 p.m. We lost about 3 hours on the way. Actual travelling, 9½ hours. Distance, 35 miles.

A few minutes after leaving, McGinnis sighted a cow moose and calf on the opposite bank of the river, a short distance downstream. Andrew and I put off in our canvas boat, and after firing four shots each, we had both. Both our first shots missed (probably owing to the rocking of the boat as we were quite near). We share equally the killing of the cow; the calf I settled with one shot. Gave half to the Hamiltons.

We stopped at one or two points and prospected. Ingraham found colors, but very fine.

While having supper, about 8 o'clock, we entered a canyon, and about ½ to 1 mile down saw a blazed tree and pulled into shore to see if it was a notice. This it turned out to be. It was left by the Hopkins party and stated that the "canyon was OK." We were fully 1½ hours running this part. The scenery was wild. Length probably about 6 miles.

We continued sailing till it was quite late in order that the Hamiltons might get a good camping place; finally we spied smoke ahead and made for it. At 10 o'clock we reached the smoke and found half a dozen parties camped, among them Judge [Morse] and Joe Millette, White and Sennett, also the Peacock party. We delivered the bag of dunnage found on the gravel bar to Dick Feltham, the owner.

According to a map owned by Spiers (of the White and Sennett party), we are at the mouth of the Lansing Creek. There are numerous signs of white men having been here. The people saw a blazed tree some miles up river with the name "Neiberg 98 Seattle Washington Ter." and one was seen in this neighbourhood dated "27 July 1898."* There is a bank off which the trees have been cut to allow tracking, also signs of camps. There cannot be any doubt now as to our whereabouts; we are certainly on the Stewart River. It appears that the big stream we passed on the left, or entered perhaps I should say, about 35 or 40 miles from Spring City (second day's travelling), was the North Fork of the Stewart.

Editor's note: It is possible that these signs could have been left by Klondikers who had come that way, via the Edmonton-Mackenzie water route, in 1897-98, although there is no indication that any came down the Stewart River. It seems more likely that they were left by miners who had penetrated that far from Dawson City.

Tuesday, May 30, 1899

Remained at the mouth of Lansing Creek all day. Several parties went up the creek this morning and expect to be away several days; they took packs with them. We leave tomorrow morning — McGinnis, Andrew, Constant and myself — for a trip; we also take packs as, judging by the mouth of the stream, it must be pretty long and we may be required to go a considerable way up and be away for several days. Ingraham found several small colors of heavy gold near the mouth, but some others claim that it is impossible to get a color 2½ to 3 miles up. They also found colors where Ingraham did, but not above. Several parties leave tomorrow morning to go down [the Stewart towards Dawson City].

Wednesday, May 31, 1899

This morning three parties — White and Sennett, Joe and Judge [Morse], and Peacock — left to continue on downstream. The four of us mentioned in yesterday's notes, left with packs at 9:30 and returned at 7:30 p.m. We met several who had started the day before on their way back, and their report was so unfavourable that we deemed it best to return and continue our trip downstream. Lansing Creek, judging it by its size, must be of considerable length; to reach its headwaters, with supplies, if we found gold, would take a long time and we would not have time to work, get sufficient [gold] (unless our claims were very rich, which the prospects at its mouth do not indicate), and leave us time to get out this Fall. During the past few days my opinion has changed somewhat, and I am now beginning to think that the lower we can get down and strike gold, the better. I have always held this opinion, but I also thought it better to prospect the headwaters, to take our chances and remain [here], as we might not strike below. But I now feel more inclined to get nearer civilization, at the risk of passing something that might prove fairly good.

Prospecting with a pack on one's back is not, by any means, easy work, particularly through such country as we passed through yesterday — muskeg, hills, bush, burnt land covered with fallen trees. We went up five miles before beginning to prospect (the river below had already been prospected by other parties with the results already mentioned). We did not find anything. The people we met coming back had been several miles beyond and had found nothing to warrant their going farther.

Will probably leave tomorrow morning.

Thursday, June 1, 1899

Weighed anchor and began drifting downstream at 11:00 a.m. and stopped at 8 p.m.: 9 hours, lost 2½ hours for meals and prospecting the mouths of three small creeks; 6½ hours drifting, at 3½ miles per hour; total, 23 miles. Would have travelled till a later hour had not the Hamiltons killed a moose at 8 p.m. which had to be dressed. They gave us half. We have now almost more meat than we can handle. I hope it does not go bad on our hands. About fifteen minutes before killing the moose, they had several shots at a black bear. I saw the gentleman [the bear] going up hill from the point where we were having supper. I thought at first that he was killed, but he got away. We hurried up and got to the place where the Hamiltons were and helped to look for the brute, but could not find it. Would have liked to have been closer to it to have had a better view.

The river still continues on its even course, without impediments. I think that we should reach the South Fork tomorrow morning, after a couple of hours sailing. Ogilvie's map shows the distance, in a straight line, between Lansing Creek and South Fork as 20 miles; allow 8 or 10 miles for bends, and say that the river between points is 28 to 30 miles, and we have covered 23 miles.

Beautiful weather.

Friday, June 2, 1899

Left anchorage at 9 a.m. and stopped at 11 p.m.: 14 hours, less 4 hours for meals and dressing three moose. We calculated the rate today at a little over three-mile an hour rate — the wind which was very strong, and upstream, checked our speed somewhat. The river continues its even course and here and there opens out into a network of channels and islands. We are now a considerable distance from the high snow-capped mountains, but get a view of them now and again. The hills in the immediate vicinity are comparatively low and fully covered with bush. During yesterday's run we passed a great deal of poplar bush. Just at 12 o'clock Henry spied a moose on the shore below and Andrew and I put off with rifles. The animal crossed the main channel and bar before I fired, and was almost off his feet and ready to swim for the main shore when I fired a shot to draw his attention. He then turned and made for the bar, stopping several times on the way. My second shot did the business and almost as soon as [the moose] got on the bar she dropped. Just about supper time we caught up the Hamiltons. We found them skinning a moose. They shot it in the bush along the shore. At about 9:30 a.m. Andrew caught sight of another moose; we took the canvas boat and made for a gravel bar — the moose was in a small opening on the main shore. We crossed the bar and fired across the inside channel. Andrew fired four and I fired three shots; my third shot dropped her in her tracks. The Hamiltons stopped on their way down (we were ahead) and took meat on board. Have decided to choose a suitable camp for drying the meat and stop for three or four days. We have now about 1000 pounds of meat on hand and must stop and dry it if we wish to save it.

Strong head winds all day; cold with a little rain.

Saturday, June 3, 1899

Did not move today and it will be well into next week before we do. We built drying frames this morning and finished cutting up and hanging meat late tonight. It will probably take four days or so to dry the meat — smudges going night and day. At supper we drew for nights [to keep the smudges going and perhaps protect the meat]. Plen handed round the hat. There were five tickets drawn in the following order:

Constant, no. 5 (or fifth night); Eben, no. 4; Andrew, no. 3; Henry, no. 2 and Charlie, no. 1. So Charlie struck first night and it is quite possible there will not be any fifth night; if so, Constant gets off "Scot free."

It has been a miserable day, a strong cold wind blowing all day and evening; now and again showers.

We are camped on a very pretty spot.

Sunday, June 4, 1899

Nothing of any consequence occurred today. The meat is drying fairly well, considering the miserable weather we are having. The sun has not "been out" for several days, except for a few minutes now and again, simply to let us know that it is still in existence.

Went down the river a short way this afternoon with Dave Hall. We took our rifles but did not see anything.

The river is gradually falling and we are hoping that it will continue to do so and soon arrive at a low level. Ingraham, yesterday, found 9 good colors on the surface of a bar opposite camp and thinks we should be slow to go down, as it is quite possible we may find something good on the bars when the water is lower.

Monday, June 5, 1899

Still in camp drying meat.

This afternoon we were somewhat surprised to see a skin boat coming down the river and at first thought it was Doc Brown, Bill George and Ferguson, but as there were five men in the boat we concluded it could not be them. When they noticed our camp they came in and we found the crew to consist of two Englishmen, Frank Braine and Jack Garnett, and three Indians.* They are two very nice fellows and have expressed a wish to travel down with us. How far we will travel together I cannot say, as they are going direct to Dawson. They left a companion at the headwaters of one of the streams running into the Stewart, and Braine is returning with the Indians and more supplies. They saw the two shacks of white men that the Wind River Indians spoke of. It appears that a man by the name of Power has been up there two or three times (he left his name and dates of visits on trees) and they cannot understand what attracted him such a long distance from the Yukon River if he did not find gold. Braine intends making enquiries at Dawson regarding this man. They prospected the headwaters of several streams without success.

Ingraham found 52 colors in one pan today.

Editor's note: Frank Braine and Jack Garnett, the former from Fort Saskatchewan and the latter from Pincher Creek, Alberta, left for the Klondike in the fall of 1897. Braine was a member of the Langworthy party and Garnett the partner of R. H. Milvain. Garnett and Milvain had reached the Gravel River when Garnett came down with a severe case of scurvy and had to be rushed back to Fort Simpson. Milvain then went his own way and Garnett joined Frank Braine, deciding to push towards the Stewart where they met McAdam. According to Milvain's journal, Garnett (who had been two years on the way) "*caught typhoid fever after arriving at Dawson and died in a few days. A better man to make a trip with would be hard to find. He was never out of temper, understood all about camping and was always anxious to do more than his share of work." (MacGregor, p. 246).*

Tuesday, June 6, 1899

We expect to finish drying the meat tonight and to leave here tomorrow. Since our arrival here the water has gone down 18 to 20 inches and still continues with a downward tendency.

Tonight was to have been my turn to stay up and keep the fires going to dry the meat, but as it is sufficiently dried now I will not stay up, but let the fires out.

Braine presented us with a beaver carcase today, and we had it for supper tonight. It went very well, although not in prime condition.

Wednesday, June 7, 1899

We left camp at 9:30 a.m. At 3:15 p.m. we reached the first rapid. Passed five rapids safely and arrived at the head of the falls (Fraser) at 5 p.m. Only one of the rapids was what might be termed rough; this was the second. We took in considerable water in two dips, probably four inches. After arriving at the falls, and before supper, we went over the portage and inspected the falls on our way back. The latest report we have heard of this river, through a Los Angeles paper, gives the fall at this point at about 35 feet and we find this drop to be about correct. Ogilvie's map states 100 to 200 feet. It was our intention to begin portaging after supper, but a heavy rain set in and prevented our doing anything. The past few days the poplars have been throwing out their leaves and the scenery today is very fresh and bright.

Thursday, June 8, 1899

It is just 6 p.m. and we are floating downstream below the Fraser Falls. We left at 5:45 p.m. At the time of making yesterday's notes we did not expect to work last night, but shortly after supper the rain ceased; we began work and worked all night, not getting through the work till 4 a.m. this morning. The portage was ½ mile long and most of it in very bad condition. We made a short cut with the supplies, but we had to haul the boats considerably farther. At times we had to wade in a foot of water and muck. It was very hard work and we were all pretty well tired out when we finished the job. We slept from 5 a.m. till 1 p.m. After having something to eat we began the work of cleaning and reloading the boat and left immediately when everything was ready. Braine and Garnett gave us a great deal of valuable assistance. We engaged the Indians and at Braine's suggestion paid them half a plug of T & B each [tobacco]. We are now below the Falls and understand we have no further impediments in our way.

Braine and Garnett, with the three Indians, left a few minutes before the Hamiltons and ourselves; they will probably travel till it is late. They are going direct to Dawson. We continued drifting till 10 p.m. Lost one hour. The current appears to be less swift than above, probably not more than 2½ miles per hour.

Fine day and the scenery beautiful.

Friday, June 9, 1899

Began drifting at 8:30 a.m. and stopped at 5 p.m. At last the last vestige of doubt as to our whereabouts has been disposed of. At 1 p.m. we struck a camp occupied by two men who had come up the river from the Yukon. The full party consisted of four, but two had gone down to Dawson "to get the latest reports." They had no late news to give us, but stated that on the 27th of August last, when they began the ascent of the river, the prospects were that 75,000 would winter at Dawson. They said that a great many had come up the river [Stewart] a long way, but that almost all had returned. "Firewood $30 a cord in Dawson." They expected to go down in three weeks as they had not struck anything. They had spent the winter hunting. They had all the fresh meat they required. Had killed five bear (trapped them). They informed us that the river was very high and all the bars were covered, and that the river is easy of ascent in low waters; also that the river running from Mayo Lake entered the Stewart 15 miles below their camp. We have about decided to stop at the mouth of Mayo (?) River till the water reaches a lower level, so that we can prospect the bars.

We prospected a small stream and bank yesterday, but prospects were very poor.

Weather unsettled and showery. We stopped at the mouth of what we supposed might be the Mayo River, but Schultz rowed up the stream and came around by the main channel, showing it to be an island.

Saturday, June 10, 1899

Began drifting at 9:30 a.m. and reached the mouth of the Mayo River at 12:10 p.m. The Hamiltons arrived at about half an hour later. Andrew and I went up the stream a short distance with the idea of prospecting, but could not reach the bars owing to high water. On our return Charlie informed us that Plen, Henry and Constant were in favor of continuing on down stream till we reached a point where men were working. After a short talk we all decided to go on, Andrew and I saying that we would prefer going on to Dawson and closing out the business [meaning absolving the partnership]. We left at 6:10 p.m. I am now indifferent to what we do and shall be glad when the end comes, so that I can begin something on my own account. I am tired of the party and everything connected with it!

Drifted till 10 o'clock p.m. Weather unsettled and showery.

Sunday, June 11, 1899

Began drifting at 7:30 a.m. and continued till 7 p.m. The current during today's run was swift, we think fully 3½ miles per hour. We lost half an hour. The appearance of the country has greatly changed — hills much lower and poplar bush has largely replaced spruce. We had a good view today of a black bear and her two cubs. We went ashore with the intention of trying for a shot, but the family skipped to new quarters and we failed to find their new address.

The day was pleasant, although the weather continues unsettled and we had a few showers.

Monday, June 12, 1899

Began drifting at 8 a.m. and stopped at 7 p.m. We lost during the day about 1½ hours, leaving 9½ hours travelling. The current is increasing and the rate today was probably 4 miles per hour.

Shortly before noon we came to quite a village of shacks, and at the time supposed them to be shacks built by miners who had wintered there, but within half an hour of leaving the place we came to an Indian encampment at the mouth of McQuestin River. There were probably about a dozen families in the place. Three miners happened to be there at the time and they informed us that the shacks above belonged to these Indians. There is quite a difference between these Indians and those on the Wind River; they have quite a Mongolian appearance, particularly some of the men. The women informed us that they had come up from below and had been up McQuestin River but had not struck anything, and that some 8 or 10 men were still at the headwaters. They estimate the distance to the mouth of the Stewart roughly at about 100 miles. About ¼ miles below the Indian encampment we saw a "free trader's" establishment, the first store of any kind that we have seen for 11 months. We did not go ashore, but spoke to the proprietor as we drifted by. Near by was a very large log building without a roof. This, we were informed, was put up by some company to be in readiness should any rich strikes be made. We passed several Indian cemeteries on the banks. The miners referred to told us that some wretched lies had gone abroad regarding two of the tributaries of the McQuestin River, one that $7,000,000 would be taken out of one creek during the winter; and that another creek was paying $500,000 a month. If the truth were known not a single "grub stake" has been taken out. I think I could stand by and enjoy the sight of seeing the tongues cut out of some of those infernal liars.

We passed a couple of other parties during the day. We spoke to one of the parties (we landed) and one of the men told us that they had worked the bar there for ten days last fall and took out $130.00 per man or $10.00 per day. They did not arrive till the first of September and were stopped by frost. This was at the mouth of Independence Creek. They said we were 73 miles up the Stewart River.

We are making grand time and will probably reach Stewart post tomorrow. What then? "God only knows!"

Tuesday, June 13, 1899

Began drifting at 8 a.m. and stopped at 12 p.m. at Stewart City; 16 hours, less 2 hours for stops.* The rate today would not probably exceed 3½ miles per hour.

On the way down we met several parties. At about noon we saw men working on a bar and put in and found Craigie and Smith, Jack Jill and Charlie Schultz and three Swedes. They had been working a day or so but owing to the high water could only do "skimming" on the top of the bar. They went down four or five feet but found nothing. The "stuff" appeared to lie on top. They were making about $1.25 to $1.40 a day per man. They expressed great regret at having rushed down the river and wished they were farther up. It is too early for bar washing.

Stewart City is almost deserted. Last summer about 6,000 were there but all have left save a few. We saw groups of shacks every here and there for quite a time before we reached the City. Made a good many enquiries about the surrounding country, but the information received was very limited and the quality uncertain. When the rush into this section occurred last year, about every yard of creek and river was staked and is still held, so that to go into a lot of hard work without knowing to what extent we would be encroaching would be folly. Later in the

128

season when the rights expire by lapse of time, it might be all right, but at present we cannot do anything.

Will probably leave for Dawson tomorrow. It was our intention to prospect Henderson Creek, but the chances are that with the above information before us, that we will pass it.

The Monkey Show is now exhibiting at Dawson City, but as they cannot give a complete show without us, we will join them as soon as possible.**

*Editor's note: McAdam is now at the junction of the Stewart and Yukon Rivers where, in fact, gold had been discovered in 1885. In 1886 about 100 miners were making a $100 a day and in that same year the trio of Harper, McQuesten and Mayo (note their names on rivers and lakes) established a trading post at the mouth of the Stewart (see Berton's Klondike, *p. 15). In the summer of 1898 the miners again flocked to the mouth of the Stewart. The community to which McAdam refers was situated on a trio of islands and boasted about fifty log cabins and hundreds of tents. "This camp," wrote one prospector, "has a population of many hundreds. It boasts a police post, a recording office, and a post office. The camp is beginning to become a town, and people are thinking of living here over the winter." (Carl Lokke,* Klondike Saga, *p. 97). McAdam's statement that there were, in the summer of 1898, nearly 6,000 men at Stewart City (and environs) was not far off the mark. But the number quickly dwindled. "Stewart River," according to* The Klondike Nugget, *"has proven anything but the gold yielder it was expected to be. Discouraged prospectors are leaving by the score, selling their outfits for what they can get, in their anxiety to get out of the country before the cold weather sets in. It is reported that outfits can be bought at the mouth of the Stewart, at very cheap rates, from men who are hastening to reach the outside." That was in August of 1898; by the time McAdam reached the "city" in 1899 it was almost deserted; the gold had run out.*

**McAdam's last remark regarding the "Monkey Show at Dawson City" is clear indication that his wry sense of humour, with the end of the long trek, is returning, but the remark has a great deal of truth in it. One has only to read chapter nine of Berton's Klondike *to affirm that truth. Dawson City (so named by William Ogilvie in 1896) was, in every sense of the word, a "boom" town. From a deserted piece of river bank it grew to a town of 6,000 inhabitants in 1896; by 1898 it had grown to 30,000 (with an equal number scattered along the nearby creeks). And "boom" prices prevailed:*

Rough log cabins rented for as much as $75.00 to $100.00 per month. Lumber ran from $100.00 to $200.00 per thousand feet; a frying chicken fetched $35.00, eggs $3.00 each, oranges from $1.00 apiece up; Bull Durham tobacco $1.00 for a five-cent sack; salt was practically worth its weight in gold, while restaurants sold mush-and-milk at $5.00 a bowl, a moose steak at $5.00 — a cucumber fetched the same price — while the ritzy Arcade Restaurant, Dawson's 'Delmonico' where waiters sported alpaca coats and balanced napkins on their arms, served canned oyster stew at $12.00 a *bowl. . . . The price of Ladue lots continued to reach astronomical figures, one corner lot having, allegedly, sold for $20,000.00. (Hinton and Godsell, The Yukon, p. 84).*

It was to this garish carnival that McAdam was headed; short of turning back, there was no place else to go.

Wednesday, June 14, 1899

Began drifting at 10 a.m. and continued till 7 p.m. We stopped earlier tonight as we wanted to get sufficient firewood to last us some time in Dawson. This is a fine large river [the Yukon], but a very slow river to travel on, unless going down stream. While at Stewart one steamer arrived, the "Mervin", a stern-wheeler — 36 hours out from Dawson. I imagine she must be one exceptionally slow boat as the boats below make good time up stream. Am figuring the rate of speed today at 5 miles an hour. We had a head wind a good part of the day and it probably checked our speed somewhat. Did not find the current as swift as we thought it was.

Thursday, June 15, 1899

"All aboard for Dawson." Began drifting at 3:30 a.m. and arrived at Dawson at 8 a.m. 4½ hours at probably a 5-mile rate. This makes the total distance from the Stewart River to Dawson 50 miles instead of 69 miles as given in the tables. This is a big difference and while we may be mistaken owing to the difficulty in telling the rate the current is travelling at, I think it is very much nearer the mark than 69 miles.

Immediately on our arrival here we went up to the Post Office to get the mail, if any, but had to wait around a long time (till 9 o'clock and our time was 1½ hours too fast) before we got in. Am I ever to receive a letter? Where are my letters? Surely the folks have written to me. Not a letter and I so anxious to hear from home and my little daughter. Will my luck ever turn?

Spent the day looking around town and what a surprise it was to see it. They say here that the place covers as much ground as Frisco. It is certainly quite a large place. No two agree on the population. Have heard figures given as high as 30,000. This, however, I think, must largely over state the number [not according to most historians]. There is one main business street along the river front, but business is not by any means confined to this street. Saloons form a good proportion of the places of business and do a rushing business. In the best class, drinks are 50c (4 bits) but in most places 25c (2 bits). A very prominent sign and one to be seen everywhere reads "Whiskey and cigars 25c".

The gambling business is run on a very extensive scale — almost every saloon has its room where all kinds of games are in full blast — faro, roulette, craps and poker. This business is permitted, of course, by law. Dance halls also do a big business and girls are there lounging around the halls and bars in sufficient numbers to afford those who want to dance an opportunity. One dollar per dance and for the man; 50c extra for the woman. The music is very good. There are some respectable women here, as in other places, but their number is small in comparison with the disreputable class.

Merchandise of all classes is fairly cheap considering the "out of the way" position of the place [the extraordinary high prices mentioned before were current during the peak of the rush in 1898; in 1899 both the numbers of miners and the prices had dropped]. When I say cheap, of course, staples are meant — flour $12.00 to $14.00 per 100; bacon 22 to 25c per pound; sugar 30c per pound (last winter $1 per pound); butter 75c per pound and so on. Ready-made boots $6 to $8.

Monday, June 19, 1899: Dawson

Hanging around doing nothing but sight seeing. Yesterday I went over to Ham Fisher's cabin. He has struck it rich — as high as $5.60 per pan. He has made us an offer of "lay" on a claim of which he is half owner. Andrew and I are thinking of going over and seeing the place. Our party is in a muddle, however, and it appears to me that matters should be straightened out and our position understood by all before any work is done. The party is too large and we do not pull together. For my part I would cancel the contract and every man go on his own account.

Tuesday, June 26, 1899

Matters are moving along in the same uncertain manner and we are not doing anything practical. Time is passing rapidly and if we are to do anything we must begin without loss of time. Maltby, McGinnis and Andrew went back to the creeks last Thursday morning and returned early yesterday morning; so far as I can learn nothing was done but view the country.

Tuesday, July 4, 1899

Today is the day the eagle screams and bands play Yankee Doodle. While I write in our tent, I hear the shouts of the crowd in Barrack Square mingled with the strains of U.S. national tunes. They are having quite a pleasant time.

Our party is now dissolved, and Andrew and myself are living alone. Henry [Chomiere] secured a job as ship's carpenter on the steamer "Cudahy" at $100 a month, room and board, and left a week ago. Constant is wandering around on his "own hook." Do not know where he is living. Charlie leaves today for home, via White Horse and Skagway. McGinnis is remaining here, but what his intentions are we do not know. I understand, however, from outside sources, that he is going home, via St. Michaels and San Francisco. The end is not an unpleasant one and we are parting good friends. We sold out all the partnership property and divided some. We realized very little. Such supplies as flour and bacon, etc., we did not sell but divided as well as we could. I expected it would not be long in coming about after we decided (while up the Stewart River) to make Dawson without doing any work on the way.

What are we to do now we are free? Look up a claim, or look for a job? Again, "time will tell." It is probable Andrew and I will go back to Last Chance Creek where Ham Fisher is located and try our luck at prospecting.

Time passes slowly here. We have been here three weeks and must now end the holiday and settle down to work, and try and make some money. Now that we are free I feel much better. Andrew and I have not formed a partnership: I for one intend to steer clear of any such entanglements. Still, later on we may find it to our natural advantage to join forces, but for the present, while we are living together, we are free to go our own ways.

Epilogue

The final outcome of this particular expedition is not unlike most others: few struck it rich; most partnerships dissolved, a few men staying to take jobs or continue searching for gold, but most returning to their home towns. Eben McAdam was one of the former.

Shortly after arriving in Dawson City, after staking a few unproductive claims, McAdam beame a clerk with the North American Transportation and Trading Company, which had become a firmly established business in the Yukon. Later he became resident manager of the company and a much-esteemed citizen of Dawson City. "There is," wrote John T. Faris in his book *Seeing Canada,* "a manager of an investment company [in Dawson City], that is not now doing business, though it has much property that needs looking after. The manager has much time at his disposal, especially in the long winter nights. But his days and nights are profitably full for he has hobbies. Ornithology is one — he has found more than fifty birds about Dawson, and astronomy is another. His beautiful brass model of the heavenly bodies, electrically driven, would be the treasure for a great university [it was, for some years, housed at McGill University]." His skill at carving, which helped pass many days on his trip to the Klondike, continued to excite admiration: "His fishing rods and rifles," states his daughter, "were things of beauty." McAdam died, on May 23, 1927, not rich, but, perhaps more important, well-loved and greatly respected in the Yukon Territory.

Andrew Smith, who was 25 at the time of the Klondike trip, also stayed in Dawson City. There he carried on a very successful brokerage business and was elected to the Yukon Territorial Council. After serving in the First World War, for which he was awarded the military cross, Smith put a fleet of steamboats on the Stikine River and became well-known as "Captain" A. W. H. Smith.

Charles Maltby, as McAdam indicates in his diary, returned to Montreal. In August, 1899, the Montreal *Star* carried his story in which Maltby stated: "I would not undergo such an expedition again for all the loose gold in the Klondike region." His disillusion, unlike McAdam's determination to make the best of it, is quite apparent: "There is not much chance of work there [in Dawson City], because the city is overcrowded with idle men, willing to work for almost anything to keep body and soul together. As for securing claims, there is not the least chance, as all the good things even up into the mountains have been staked out by men who are barely eking out a living. . . . My advice to prospective prospectors is 'keep away from the Klondike.' "

All we know of Henry Chomiere is what McAdam tells us in his diary; neither McAdam nor Maltby mention what happened to McGinnis, except both say he stayed in Dawson City.

We will let Eben McAdam have the last word, especially since that last word is such a contrast to Maltby's pessimistic assessment. In a letter written to his parents-in-law shortly after arriving at Dawson City, McAdam summed up his experience: "Some men thought (I don't know why) that all they had to do was to come to this place and they would have their fortunes fly into their arms. Poor fools! What a disappointment! I do not regret the trip, however, and intend giving the place and surroundings a trial. The trip has cost me a lot of time and a little money, but I still have hopes of making a stake, however small. If I do not succeed I will have to be satisfied with the experience." That was spoken like a true Klondiker.

Bibliography*

Berton, Pierre. "Gold Rush Writing: The Literature of the Klondike." *Canadian Literature 14* (1962): 85-100.

Berton, Pierre. *Klondike: The Life and Death of the Last Great Gold Rush.* Toronto: McClelland & Stewart, 1958.

Corp, A. "The Trail of '98 by the Gravel River Route." *Arctic Circular*, March 1959, pp. 35-51.

Cresswell, R. H. S. "Inland Trail to the Klondike." *Alaska Sportsman* 29 (1963): nos. 2-3, 5-8, 10-11.

Graham, Angus. *The Golden Grindstone: The Adventures of George M. Mitchell.* Toronto: Oxford University Press, 1935.

Hemstock, C. Anne and Geraldine A. Cooke. *Yukon Bibliography: Update 1963-1970.* Edmonton: Boreal Institute, 1973.

Lokke, C. L. *Klondike Saga.* Minneapolis: University of Minnesota Press, 1965.

Lotz, James R. *Yukon Bibliography: Preliminary Edition.* Ottawa: Department of Northern Affairs, 1964.

MacGregor, J. G. *The Klondike Rush Through Edmonton.* Toronto: McClelland & Stewart, 1970.

Murray, Alexander H. *Journal of the Yukon 1847-48.* Edited by L. J. Burpee. Ottawa: Government Printing Bureau, 1910.

Ogilvie, William. *The Klondike Official Guide.* Toronto: Hunter, Rose, 1898.

Slobodin, R. "The Dawson Boys: Peel River Indians and the Klondike Gold Rush." *Polar Notes*, June 1963, pp. 24-35.

*For the interested reader, there are many excellent sources (both secondary and primary) dealing with the Klondike gold rush. I have listed only those which I have used in editing McAdam's diary. Titles of others may be found in the Berton, Lotz and Hemstock bibliographies listed above. — ED.